Using the Newspaper to Teach Language Arts

For middle grades and up

Marilyn Olson

DALE SEYMOUR PUBLICATIONS

Illustrations: Alison McKinley
Cover design: Mark McGeoch

Copyright © 1984 by Dale Seymour Publications. All rights reserved.
Printed in the United States of America. Published simultaneously in
Canada.

The worksheets in this book were originally published in daily
newspapers, with major support coming from the Eugene *Register-Guard*
and from other newspapers throughout Oregon, in Savannah, Georgia,
and in Richmond, Virginia. Each activity appeared individually under the
title "Newschool, Learning from Life," copyright 1979 by Lane Education
Service District, and copyright 1980, 1981, 1982 by Newschool.

Limited reproduction permission. The publisher grants permission to
reproduce up to 100 copies of the worksheets in this book for
noncommercial classroom or individual use. Any further duplication is
prohibited.

Order number DS03412
ISBN 0-86651-205-5

CONTENTS

Preface/v
How to Use This Book/vii

TEACHING NOTES
Language Skills/T-1 Reading Comprehension/T-5 Written Composition/T-10
Literary Themes/T-14 Nonverbal Communication/T-19

Part 1 LANGUAGE SKILLS
Bookmaking/1 Grocery List/2 Names and News Words/3 Alphabetical Orders/4
Character Analysis/5 Key Words/6 Word Webs/7 Prefixing!/8 Suffixed/9
Syl-la-bles/10 Big (Voluminous) Words/11 Oppo-Words/12 Common and Proper
Names/13 Action!/14 Synonyms & Antonyms/15 Fooling Around/16
Skim & Scan/17 Onomatopoeia/18 Acronyms Etc./19 Generally Speaking/20
Scrambled Stories/21 Types of Sentences/22 Word Search/23 Double Meaning/24
Works of Art/25

Part 2 READING COMPREHENSION
Exaggeration/26 Making Comparisons/27 The Famous 4 W's/28 The Big Ideas/29
Simply Say It!/30 Once Upon a Time/31 Comprehension Clues/32 Writing for a
Reason/33 Facts and Opinions/34 One Person's Opinion/35 Viewpoints/36
Two Sides to Every Story/37 Read and React/38 I'm Against It/39 Dear Editor/40
Agree-Disagree/41 "Beauty"/42 Setting/43 Static & Dynamic Characters/44
Beginning and Ending/45 Presuming & Predicting/46 Suspense!/47 To Be Continued/48

Part 3 WRITTEN COMPOSITION
Sentencing!/49 Playing with Words/50 Sensitivity/51 Sentence Combining/52
A Funny Thing Happened/53 Paragraphs—Easy as ABC/54 No Two Alike/55
Making Sense/56 Read On! Read On!/57 Create-a-Character/58 Fact & Fiction/59
Fact & Fantasy/60 Rhyme & Reason/61 The Heart of the Matter/62 Good Senses/63
The Five Senses/64 Faces with Feelings/65 From Start to Finish/66 Lost & Found/67
You Are There/68 You're Kidding/69 Whadja Say?/70 Mixed Up/71

Part 4 LITERARY THEMES
Struggle/72 Struggle and Strife/73 Mishaps and Other Misfortunes/74 Choosing
Our Responses/75 Good Ones & Bad Ones/76 Change of a Lifetime/77 Ups and
Downs/78 Turning Points/79 Meanness vs. Courage/80 He-roes and Her-oes/81
Heroic Action/82 Help for the Hapless/83 Desire and Determination/84 Good
Sports/85 Success/86 What Families Are For/87 Personal Profiles/88 Virtues of
a Valentine/89 Mother's Day/90 Father's Day/91 The Way I See Me/92 Free
Advice/93 Candid Comics/94 Laughing Matter/95

Part 5 NONVERBAL COMMUNICATION
Louder Than Words/96 Lettering/97 Line Drawings/98 Creative Creations/99
Color Added/100 Warm and Cool Colors/101 Sign Language/102 Trademarks/103
The Art of Persuading/104 Looks on Faces/105 Masks/106 Costumes/107
Characters/108 Lively Bodies/109 Tricks and Techniques/110 Kinds of Cartoons/111
Details, Details/112 Slight (?!) Exaggerations/113 Cartoons That Comment/114
Cartoon Comparisons/115 Opinionated Pictures/116 Foto Facts/117 Just Picture
That!/118

Acknowledgments

NewsSchool owes its existence

- to Lane Education Service District, where the idea of creating 365 newspaper activities was conceived and encouraged.

- to hundreds of Lane County (Oregon) teachers, whose classrooms served as labs, whose students served as lab assistants, and whose good ideas and suggestions helped greatly in the revision and rewriting of the original set of activities.

- to several astute newspaper publishers across the country, who purchased the activities, published them daily in their papers, and promoted their use in classrooms.

- To Alison McKinley, whose apt and adroit art gave life and added meaning to the activities.

- To Sue Bishop, who typed and pasted and filed and sorted and mailed and recorded and kept it all together.

- To Ken and Tim and Matt, who helped the author believe it could and should be done.

PREFACE

The dilemmas of teaching and learning in the Information Age include these: (1) that there is always more than we need to know, about more things than we could possibly want to know about, and (2) that lacking the necessary motivation to push the button, change the channel, or turn the page, we are usually left wishing that we knew *more* about some things and *less* about other things.

The activities in this publication are designed to help teachers and students achieve three important Information Age goals:

1. *To access information of significance and interest.* Information is of no value unless we choose to pay attention to it. There are people who choose *not* to know, *not* to read, *not* to search out information. But most of our students really *do* want to know more about what is going on in the world. Schools need to provide them the time and the right environment for discovering that world, talking about how it works, questioning those who are making things happen, and identifying their own role in the world scene.

2. *To process information efficiently and accurately.* Information is of no value unless we know how to make sense of it: how to decode the symbols, how to add things up, how to eliminate the irrelevant, and how to understand the terms used. As students master "information processing skills," they will be able to discern meaning in the mass of information available to them. There is a further demand, too: that they be able to process that information even while life is continuously moving and changing.

3. *To gain new knowledge from the assimilation of information.* Information is of no particular value unless it extends what we already know, unless we learn something new. Students must do more than simply pay attention to it; they must do more than understand it at a literal level. They must be able to *do* something with the information they read: organize it in a different way, classify it, compare it, find similarities and differences, look for its origins, predict its future.

Today's news reports are inaccurate and incomplete—not intentionally so (as may be the case in a country with no free press), but because that is the nature of news. News *develops*, day by day. Stories unfold; reporters continue to dig; the facts come out slowly—or events occur quite suddenly, and it takes days to reconstruct what really happened. That's why we can believe with some confidence that there is no better record of what went on in the world yesterday—overseas, across the continent, downtown—than what is contained in today's newspaper. The additions and corrections will appear in tomorrow's paper or the next day's, as a letter to the editor, a news item, an editorial, an ad, or as a new development in the ongoing drama we call Life. The newspaper is a place to learn that *every day* counts. There will always be more to know.

As teachers, we are more accustomed to presenting textbook information, which is usually two to three years old by the time it reaches the student. All the answers are there. At any point we can ask *who, what, where, when,* or *why*, and expect to get the "right" answers.

Journalists, meanwhile, are asking the same questions: *who, what, where, when, why*—because they do not already know the answers. Everyday, they write up answers to those questions from thousands of different sources, on hundreds of subjects, and print them in newspapers. What they discover and report, in time, changes textbook content. As a "textbook" itself, the newspaper is updated every day.

What, then, is THE CURRICULUM we ought to be offering our students? A limited body of knowledge to be transmitted? Or an *unlimited* amount of information just waiting to be discovered, processed, used, made meaningful? These *NewsSchool* activities are based on the conviction that the curriculum is LIFE in its broadest sense; that it is constantly changing; and that certain skills, when applied to real-life information, will lead to worthwhile learning.

Each of the activities emphasizes a *process*—steps or tasks that students complete in order to arrive at some new level of understanding or learning. In addition, each of the activities emphasizes *content*—a certain kind of information to be processed. This merging of *predictable* process with *unpredictable* content creates an excitement lacking in other forms of learning; it is perhaps the best argument for using the newspaper in the classroom.

HOW TO USE THIS BOOK

What's in the NewsSchool book?

The core of this book consists of 118 reproducible worksheets, designed for use with students in the middle grades and up—including high school and adult education classes. A quick look through the contents page will show that the activities fall into five basic classifications:
1. Language Skills
2. Reading Comprehension
3. Written Composition
4. Literary Themes
5. Nonverbal Communication

Obviously these will apply most directly to language arts, reading, and literature classes, but art and social studies teachers, too, will find activities in this book that are appropriate to their teaching goals.

In fact, because the news content itself is often subject-oriented (most commonly in the areas of social studies, science, and health), the skills needed for reading, understanding, and responding to the substance of an article are usually interdisciplinary.

At its most basic level, *NewsSchool* can help provide a structure for regular newspaper reading that will build good reading habits. Regular use of the *NewsSchool* activities will develop skills in these areas:
1. Comprehension of written material at the literal, interpretive, critical, and creative levels.
2. Understanding of local, national, and international events and issues as they pertain to the life of the individual citizen.
3. Practical application of basic educational skills and concepts.
4. Discerning the roles and responsibilities of the free press as a reliable information resource.

A section of teaching notes that precedes the worksheets offers ideas for presenting each activity to your class. These notes alert you to important considerations and the occasional pitfall, and sometimes suggest possibilities for extending the activity into a larger project. The answer to the *Bonus!* question on each worksheet is also included in these notes.

To select appropriate activities, familiarize yourself with what's available by skimming through the notes and the worksheets. In doing so, teachers usually discover that certain activities trigger ideas for use, either because of their relevancy to a particular current news event, or because of their application to the teacher's curricular needs.

What's the scope of a single activity?

Each *NewsSchool* activity takes the reader through a step-by-step process of reading and thinking. The first steps of each activity involve fairly simple tasks of locating and recognizing certain types of information found in newspapers. From there, the activity proceeds to increasingly difficult tasks of interpretation, critical evaluation, and creative thinking.

Typically, an activity will follow a three- or four-step pattern something like this:

1. find, list, count, identify a certain kind of news item, language form, or topic;
2. read and offer your interpretation of sequence, cause and effect, relationships, roles;
3. evaluate, compare, recommend, decide something about the material selected;
4. imagine, design, illustrate, rewrite, rearrange, create something based on the material selected.

The step-by-step format may give the appearance of over-simplification. Experience with the program, however, has shown that the newspaper content itself is usually fairly complex for students. Thus, breaking the comprehension and evaluation tasks into simpler steps is extremely beneficial.

All students can profit by completing the easier first steps of an activity. Capable students will be able to finish any activity they begin. (Keep in mind that the "completion" of any activity may stop short of all the steps outlined on the worksheet, depending on the pertinence of the material available in any day's newspaper.)

In most cases, students may leave the activity at any step and still benefit from having learned something they probably did not know before. When a student or entire class pursues an activity to completion, however, they will end up producing something that reflects their own feelings and convictions—an invaluable experience in melding new information to the knowledge they already have.

Be aware of the tremendous potential in each activity. A particular worksheet may focus on verbs, or on characterization, or on symbols, but when students apply that activity to today's news events, chances are they will be learning far more. It's impossible to predict what that extra learning will be, because we never know what will appear in tomorrow's paper. For this reason, doing the same activity two or three days in a row, with successive newspapers, might produce quite different results, with different kinds of learning. Similarly, doing the same activity with several different newspapers, including some from distant cities, may also have some unexpected benefits.

Does each student need a worksheet? And what sort of work should I expect from my students?

Although each activity is presented as a worksheet, it is often neither necessary nor advisable to provide a copy for *every* student. One sheet shared by a team of several students will give them the directions they need;

students can then complete the work on their own paper or in a group display.

In fact, many activities are best displayed on another sheet of paper, on large poster board, or on a bulletin board. (Newspaper clippings frequently do not fit neatly on 8½ by 11 paper.) Colored construction paper can be a tremendous boon to the display of student work, because newsprint by itself or on white notebook paper does not look particularly exciting, and students are generally more motivated if they can be proud of their finished projects.

Although certainly appropriate for individual use, the *NewsSchool* activities are especially well suited to *teamwork*. This cannot be emphasized too much. Newspaper content is often controversial, complex, even incomplete. The inquiry/discovery process that we follow as we study emerging news may at first produce anxiety in students who aim to "do well" and "be *right*." Allowing students to work in teams, discuss ideas, and share opinions will probably heighten their interest and improve results, too.

Students who become interested in a news topic may be motivated to extend the activity into a larger project—either individual or group—involving research, data gathering, and analysis. Likewise, the product of any activity may evolve into a fairly sophisticated oral or written presentation. Some suggestions for extended projects appear in the teaching notes for the worksheets.

How much time should I allow for each activity?

The time requirements for these activities will vary greatly, and may depend on the particular newspaper you are using. For the best gauge of time, *try the activity yourself*. See how difficult it is to find the kind of article or example asked for. See what kinds of questions come up as you work through the steps. Be prepared to show the students what *you* did with the activity (assuming they will not try to duplicate your work because they will have a different newspaper). Talk about what you learned when you did the activity: what surprised you, what stumped you, what decisions you had to make, what questions it raised.

If time is limited (and it often is), consider selecting ahead of time certain articles or examples for all students to use. This will not only save time, it will help you anticipate questions and problems students may encounter, and it will help you control the outcome of the activity.

How often should I use the newspaper?

Like any good teaching resource, too much of it will defeat the purpose. Vary its use: on some days, give every student the opportunity to turn newspaper pages; on other days, pass out clippings you have selected ahead of time. The frequency of use will vary depending on the subject you teach, the level of your students, and your objectives. Most important, students should recognize through your modeling that the newspaper is a major source of current and important information and opinion.

Teachers generally use the *NewsSchool* activities in one of two ways: either they use them to teach a *newspaper unit*, aimed at helping students understand what a newspaper is and how it works, or they use them to reinforce concepts and skills related to a specific part of the curriculum. In the first instance, the newspaper itself is what's being taught, and you will likely use it often in the course of the unit. In the second instance, the newspaper is simply a tool you are teaching with; you will use it only as often as it augments and enhances your teaching goal.

Many teachers order a newspaper for their classroom so that every day, they *know* that they can depend on the newspaper as a teaching resource if nothing else is working or available.

How can I get classroom sets of newspapers?

Most daily and weekly newspapers have heard of the Newspaper in Education Program, sponsored by the American Newspaper Publishers Association (ANPA) Foundation. They are supportive of teachers' efforts to make the newspaper a regular teaching resource. Call your local newspaper and ask about their NIE services, including school subscription rates. Usually you can get classroom sets of newspapers delivered to the school for half price, or free if you are willing to take day-old issues and pick them up.

How many should I order?

Most of the activities in this book do not require that every student have a newspaper—or even that every student have the same newspaper. Keep in mind that your students will benefit from working together in teams of two or three. The newspaper is highly unpredictable, and students often rely on the supporting ideas of their group as they move through the increasingly difficult steps of the activities.

If you are in a school setting where the students change classrooms each period, you will want fresh newspapers for each class. If you have 75–100 students in three or four classes of ninth grade English or social studies, for example, you might order 10–15 newspapers for each class period. That way, each team of students will have a new paper to work with.

What about the mess that newspapers create?

Don't give the entire newspaper to students unless the activity calls for the entire paper. By using different sections of the paper each day, you can make one issue last for an entire week. If the activity calls for the front page only, spend the first few minutes of class tearing or cutting the front page from the rest of the paper and returning all but the front page to a stack of papers to be used the next day.

On days when students are using large sections of the paper, plan to spend some time in cleaning up, stacking, and discarding used newspapers. One school has a newspaper recycling bin in the parking lot. Another school tries to coordinate newspaper study with papier-mâché projects.

Dealing with the used newspapers is only one part of the mess, however. The other is the ink that rubs off on students' hands. Invest in some containers of moistened towelettes for days when students are heavily involved in finding and cutting items from the paper. Such towelettes are relatively inexpensive and are frequently available at a reduced price.

What about the sensitive material I don't want students to read?

As we've recommended before, *try the activity yourself* before asking students to do it. The appearance of the activities is sometimes deceiving. They may *look* easy and straightforward, but coupled with today's news, the match might produce a disastrous teaching situation. Let's say you are prepared to have the students do "Free Advice" (page 93). You intend to suggest that they use "Dear Abby" or a similar column as a starting place. Check the feature columns for the newspaper you will be using, just to make sure that you're willing and prepared for students to deal with the given problems in the way that the activity suggests.

Experience with students at all grade levels has shown that they can handle a wide range of topics from the news with great maturity and responsibility, because they realize that the topic is *real life*, and that its presentation in the newspaper is intended to inform, warn, raise awareness, present possibilities, influence convictions, and (it is hoped) lead to a wiser, stronger, more involved citizenry. Young people welcome the opportunity to discuss topics of importance and interest that in some way touch their own lives.

I don't always feel qualified to discuss or teach about things that appear in the newspaper. Won't that jeopardize my leadership and authority in the classroom?

Part of your philosophy for using the newspaper in the classroom should be that there is more to know than anyone can possibly know, and that new knowledge is being discovered daily. Our job as teachers is to facilitate learning—our own as well as that of our students. When you use the newspaper as a textbook, you will be learning along with the class. Your training and expertise as teacher will be evidenced by your ability to help students discover how to learn, how to share knowledge, and how to make connections and find new meaning in the things they already know and the things that are only now being discovered and reported.

TEACHING NOTES

Language Skills

Bookmaking — page 1

This creative activity uses the newspaper as a source of words and a source of ideas. Students learn from the process of arranging their clippings and pages in a meaningful sequence. At the same time, they are creating a product to be proud of. The books your students produce may be used as gifts or as teaching material. The content and the size of the books should be dictated by your objectives: the focus may simply be on alphabetical order, or it may be on recognizing more sophisticated language concepts such as metaphors or acronyms.

Bonus! A bibliomaniac is crazy about books; a bibliophile just loves them.

Grocery List — page 2

A fairly simple two-step activity for putting words in alphabetical order. If your students have access to a computer and a simple word processing program, they can do the task more efficiently that way than with paper and pencil. The exercise can become a test of speed and accuracy in "filing" information.

Given the challenge to devise an efficient way to alphabetize without the inconvenience of erasures, students may think to write the words on separate cards or slips of paper—an approach that would make the job of classifying and sequencing easier.

Bonus! This is an exercise in fluency and classification. Encourage students to see how many s-foods they can think of on their own before consulting the grocery ads. Possible answers include: salad dressing, salami, salmon, sardines, sauerkraut, scallops, sherbet, shrimp, sole, soufflé, soup, soy beans, spaetzle, spaghetti, spareribs, squash, steak, stew, strawberries, strudel, stuffing, succotash, sukiyaki, sweet potatoes, Swiss cheese.

Names and News Words — page 3

Another fairly easy activity that requires the student to know the alphabet. It also asks students to develop and accurately use a system for comparing information in two places—all the letters of the alphabet, and all the words they have selected from the newspaper. The challenge of the activity, then, is not substance so much as *process*: the organization and management of data.

Bright students may catch on early to the idea that if their name starts with A or T, it won't help them much to write down words like *an* or *the* on their first list. They will look instead for the longest words they can find—and in so doing may discover words they have never seen before.

Bonus! Many people are surprised to learn that they use more than half the alphabet in writing their full signature.

Alphabetical Orders — page 4

This activity asks students to practice alphabetizing to the second and third letter. In the process, students may discover and learn words they did not previously know. However, the main focus of learning here is on the process and the skill of dealing accurately with specific information. Neatness and perfect spelling are critical. To prove that point, ask students to prepare their lists in the three columns, then exchange papers to put someone else's words in alphabetical order. Complaints will surface quickly if the words in the lists are hard to read or if the student assigned to ordering does not agree with the spelling given.

Discuss with the students why qualities of neatness and accuracy are important in offices and businesses of all types: important information could be lost forever if it is not filed correctly, and terrible mistakes might result when information is not recorded accurately.

Bonus! Alpha is the first letter of the Greek alphabet, symbolized by the letter A.

Character Analysis   page 5

Ads work especially well for this activity because they tend to be both descriptive and positive; for example, *captivating* townhouse, *spectacular* sale. Students just learning to identify parts of speech may have trouble with the frequent use of nouns for description in news stories; for example, *telephone* interview, *sales* tax, *re-election* campaign. Encourage them to look for adjectives that could be used to describe people.

Bonus! Be aware that we are all deeply influenced by the words used to describe us. Encourage students to select for their own initials *positive* descriptive words that reflect the qualities they value most in themselves.

Key Words   page 6

While this activity is, on its most basic level, an alphabetizing drill, it leads to much more than that. First students must identify the main story in the newspaper, usually appearing in the upper right corner or across the top of the front page. In step 1, students circle words based on their alphabetical arrangement, but the heart of the activity is in step 2, where students analyze the role those words play in the story.

Key words are those that define and describe the people, places, and actions of the news event. They reflect not only the substance of the story, but the significance and consequence of the event as well. If several students are doing the same activity with the same newspaper, there could be some lively discussion about which words each student selected as key words, and why.

Bonus! Probably the elements we see first in a picture are the "what" of the event or the "who," both of which would most likely be represented by *nouns*. (Students could present an arguable case for *verbs* in action sports pictures or *adjectives* in particularly evocative shots.)

Word Webs   page 7

This activity can be as structured or creative as you permit. If the title of a student's web is *four-syllable words*, you can make an evaluation of the chosen words readily and objectively. If, however, a student chooses a more abstract title like *War*, the selection of words will reflect the student's own interpretations of that idea. Reserve judgment about any student's word choices until the student has a chance to present his or her reasons for those choices.

In any case, it is the process of classification—finding the connecting thread between all the words—that gives meaning to the activity.

Bonus! There are at least three titles that we might give to a word web containing the words *dogs* and *cats: Four-Letter Words, Animals*, and *Pets*. Accept any other classification that students can justify.

Prefixing!   page 8

Students usually realize early in the activity the difficulty of identifying prefixes. For example, *re-* can be a prefix, but is it a prefix in the word *regional*? *Em-* can be a prefix, but is it a prefix in the word *embassy*?

Step 3 of the activity can be enriched further by asking students to write definitions or synonyms for the words they have created, using the Bonus question and cartoon as an example.

Bonus! "Unfix" might mean *break, dismantle, destroy, undo, disconnect*... See how many different words students think of.

Suffixed   page 9

Before students begin this activity, they may find it interesting to predict the answer to the question in step 2: which suffix is most common in the newspaper? Students should also provide a rationale for their prediction; for example, that *-ed* will be common because the news is a report of past events.

As an extension for step 3, ask students how changing a suffix on a particular word in a news story could affect the meaning of the story. For example, "Man eats mice" has a very different meaning from "Man-eating mice."

Bonus! The fix*er* fix*ed* the fix*ture*. Notice how different suffixes can change a verb to a noun.

Syl-la-bles   page 10

Students will discover quickly how easy it is to find one-, two-, three-, and four-syllable words. Five- and six-syllable words are somewhat more difficult to find, and words of seven (or more) syllables are a rarity. Students may become frustrated by the "impossibility" of finding words with large numbers of syllables, but in their frustration, they often make some interesting observations about word construction, vocabulary, readability, word divisions, and so forth.

Bonus! *Supercalifragilisticexpialidocious*, the word made famous by Walt Disney Studios in the movie *Mary Poppins*, has fourteen syllables. It means "very good" or "very, *very* good."

Big (Voluminous) Words   page 11

The assumption in this activity is that a word of ten or more letters will most likely contain a prefix or suffix.

You might use this activity as the basis for collecting vocabulary words over a period of time. While students may assume that words of many letters are usually difficult or unfamiliar, this activity can demonstrate that such is often not the case. By the time students have identified and removed the prefix and suffix, what remains may be a very simple, familiar word. Note, for example, the words *repeatedly* and *unidentified*.

Bonus! "Ratification" means approval.

Oppo-Words   page 12

Compound words are easily found in most news stories and advertisements. The fun of the activity is in creating, defining, and using brand-new, handcrafted words. Manipulating and changing words this way reinforces the idea that people control language; language does not need to control people. In making new words, students experience their own creativity and discover one aspect of the power of communication.

Bonus! The word *today* in step 1 would qualify as a compound word.

Common and Proper Names   page 13

Students practice recognizing proper nouns and renaming them with common nouns. Some of the capitalized words on the front page will be names of local people whose positions and roles are not known to students; other proper nouns may be names of unfamiliar organizations or agencies. In these cases, encourage students to do some research in order to supply an *accurate* less specific name.

Bonus! The word *English* is a proper noun and should always be capitalized, even though the other listed school courses are not. (When naming school subjects, only other language courses—Spanish, French, German, Latin—are also capitalized.)

Action!   page 14

If you want the object of this activity to be recognizing verbs, students will need to distinguish between verbs used as verbs and verb forms used as nouns, adjectives, and adverbs. For example, "...his victory *foiled* his opponent's bid for the championship ... he left, *muttering* ..." Only one of the action words here—*foiled*—is a verb. *Muttering* is a verbal used as an adjective. Help the students test for verbs: "he foiled ... he muttering ... " This way students can quickly see which word *is* what he did and which word *describes* what he did.

If you prefer that the object of the activity be simply to strengthen word choice and enhance writing, allow the students to select *any* lively words—verbs or verbals—to work with.

Bonus! The verb *threatened* is least like the others, all of which denote actual abuse.

Synonyms & Antonyms   page 15

Students could benefit from some discussion and a few examples before starting this activity. Alert them to the idea that simple function words like *but* and *an* should not be selected, nor should proper nouns.

As the students select words, they should circle them in the newspaper in addition to writing them on their worksheet. That way, they can go back later and read the headlines with the synonyms and antonyms inserted. A point for discussion: What happens to the original meaning when we play around with the words?

Step 3 of the activity may not be as easy as it looks. The sports writer may sometimes use a predicate adjective such as "was victorious" as a way of saying that someone won. Students may find that such phrases are used more often than other verbs in place of the words *won* and *lost*.

Bonus! *Escape* and *capture* are antonyms—words that have opposite meanings.

Fooling Around   page 16

The descriptive terms used in most real estate ads are carefully selected to attract buyers. Although the use of such words may not qualify as *exaggeration*, their use often can be considered *euphemism*.

Students at higher grade levels may need encouragement to avoid listing inappropriate or crude antonyms. They should try to select words that might be used in an objective or honest appraisal of a piece of property.

As an extension, suggest that students follow up by taking snapshots (or finding pictures in real estate brochures) of the property described, to demonstrate what the ad meant by *unique*, or *cozy*, or *formal*.

Bonus! Probably no one would want the house described by antonyms—unless, of course, the price was adjusted. As a follow-up, have a student talk to a realtor about the language used in ads, and find out how much difference there might be in price between a "unique" home and a "generic" home.

Skim & Scan   page 17

Depending on the season, many of the words listed in this activity may not appear in the sports section. To increase student interest and give them more practice in skimming, ask them to prepare a similar list of their own, using sports words that appear in their copy of a current paper. When students exchange their lists and newspapers, they will know that every word on the given list *can* be found—*if* they are good skimmers!

Bonus! Professional athletes may take their playing more seriously because they are being paid to play, but *anyone* who wants to achieve excellence in sports will work at developing the skills and knowledge necessary for success.

Onomatopoeia   page 18

"Sound words" are not easy to find in headlines or ads. Students may confuse them with strong emotional words like *chill, applaud,* and *terror.* If this happens, use those strong words to trigger ideas for closely related "sound" words. For example, *chill* could trigger the word *shiver; applaud* might suggest *clap; terror* could evoke *scream.*

An extension of the activity is suggested by the Bonus question. Students could cut out words or designs from ads that evoke an emotional response in the reader, then use those to create a poetic or dramatic message.

Bonus! The color, size, arrangement, or design of letters can attract readers and cause them to stop and pay attention, almost as if the words were shouting at them.

Acronyms Etc.   page 19

Acronyms and initials can be readily found in news stories. As a rule, reporters will not use an acronym in a news story until after the full name has appeared, unless the initials are very well-known or appear elsewhere in the same paper. In some cases, we become so familiar with an acronym that we rarely think about the words it represents; for example, FBI or NBC.

Bonus! It is a popular notion that the word *news* is an acronym for North, East, West, and South. The idea is clever but not true. According to the Oxford English Dictionary, the word *news* has been in common use since the 1500s and came from the medieval term *nova* which means "a new thing."

Generally Speaking . . .   page 20

Because newspaper reports give specific information, it should not be difficult for students to supply the specific words for step 1 of the activity. General terms will be more difficult to find, but the value of seeing words renamed is important. Emphasize that students must find and cut out the words *from the paper*, not just write them from their own knowledge.

Follow up the worksheet by asking students to make their own lists of specific words found in a current newspaper. They can then exchange their lists of specifics and supply from their own knowledge a more general term. This extension will familiarize students with the important names, places, and organizations that have major roles in current events. Encourage students to move up the ladder of abstraction one rung at a time: if the specific name is Alberto Salazar, a more general term to describe him might be *marathon runner*—which would be better than the very general term *man.*

Bonus! The term *President* is most specific and further describes a kind of *leader.* Students may think that *human* is the most general since *male* is a specific human, but in fact *male* is more general because many different kinds of mammals are male, but only one kind of mammal is human.

Scrambled Stories   page 21

Similar to the idea of sequencing comic-strip segments, this activity calls for students to sequence segments of a news story, relying on punctuation, wording, or sentence sense to supply cues. If students select high-interest feature stories that won't be outdated soon, you might have the story segments laminated with clear contact paper so they can be used again and again by other students.

Bonus! *B* is the right choice because it meaningfully completes the sentence that begins the story.

Types of Sentences   page 22

Students should be able to locate all four types of sentences in the paper. Exclamatory sentences abound on the comics page, and the front page is dominated by declarative sentences. The editorial page alone usually contains all four types, especially if there are emotional letters to the editor.

For higher-level students, extend the activity to finding examples of simple, compound, complex, and compound-complex sentences.

Bonus! When a witness is interrogated, he or she gets lots of *questions*. Point out the relationship between *interrogative* sentences and the verb *interrogate*.

Word Search   page 23

Headline-writing resembles the clipped style of telegrams or classified ads. The writer tries to capture as much meaning as possible with the fewest words. The point of this activity is to study how sentences are constructed and how language is manipulated to make the writing effective. Students may become more aware of word functions by seeing the same words used as both verbs and nouns or nouns and adjectives.

Bonus! There are a number of ways that the headline could be translated into a complete sentence. Here is one suggestion: "Bicycle sales in the United States have exceeded one billion dollars during the last year." (fifteen words vs. the original nine).

Double Meaning   page 24

We can become so accustomed to the figurative meaning of words and phrases that we might overlook the phenomenon of change in language unless we are encouraged to find and analyze actual examples. Students may find it difficult to supply the literal meaning for some phrases because the figurative is so familiar. Others will be easier. For example, when a sports team "bites the dust," it means literally that they put their teeth into the dirt. Figuratively, it means that they lost or went down in defeat. Wherever possible, students should be encouraged to find a reasonable relationship between the literal and the figurative.

Bonus! An *idiom* is an expression unique to a culture and not directly translatable into other languages, such as "selldown sale" or "walk-a-thon."

Works of Art   page 25

The things that people create often reflect values that are important to them. When homes are called *beautiful, unique, spacious, immaculate,* or *charming*, that tells us something about the people who designed or decorated them. Personal qualities are also represented in dramatic, musical, or artistic performances that are reported to be *pure, spontaneous, beautiful, striking,* or *intricate*.

Note that a weekend paper may be more likely to carry fine arts reviews, unless there is a special section or a specific weekday when the newspaper features the arts.

Bonus! It is true that *all* these men were talented artists. Norman Rockwell, an American illustrator, is best known for his paintings of everyday people for magazine covers. Grant Wood, another American, is known for his paintings of the rural Midwest, the most famous being "American Gothic." Winston Churchill, an Englishman famous as one of the greatest statesmen in world history, was also a noted painter and gave several exhibitions of his work. Rembrandt, perhaps the Netherlands' greatest artist from the 17th century, is best known for his genius in portraying human emotion.

Reading Comprehension

Exaggeration   page 26

A good place to begin looking for exaggeration is in advertisements. Words like *sensational* and phrases like *unheard of savings* suggest extremes. The activity requires the student to think about the use of words in relation to the exact item or idea they describe. Almost every editorial cartoon employs exaggeration, either *directly* in overstatements in art or *indirectly* by presenting overstated opinions to make a point.

This activity could help you introduce the literary device of *hyperbole*. The activity actually involves semantic analysis, a study of intent and meaning in language.

Bonus! Discuss the Bonus with the entire class to establish what is expected. To help students get started, ask them to think about what people say when they are low on money, very hungry, very tired, or highly angered by something.

Teaching Notes: Reading Comprehension

Making Comparisons   page 27

This activity asks students to analyze similes or analogies in order to understand what the writer means. Figurative language is so common that we often do not think about the literal meaning of what is being said. Be sure students understand the difference between literal and figurative meaning. Introduce the terms *metaphor*, *simile*, and *analogy*.

Students may have trouble stating the comparison as required in step 2, especially if this is the first experience they have had in analyzing double meanings. However, trying to write them out will help students clarify their thinking.

Bonus! "One team almost beat another" is the intended answer. You may need to discuss this further with students not attuned to sports jargon.

The Famous 4 W's   page 28

The task here appears to be quite simple until you try it! Students may begin to ask, "Which *who* should I underline?" There often seem to be two or more *who*'s in a news story. Generally, *who* is the subject of the story, *what* is the verb and object, and *when* and *where* are adverbs: A 15-year-old boy (*who*) accidentally injured his best friend in a shooting accident (*what*) on Wednesday (*when*), 15 miles north of the city (*where*). Notice that "his best friend" is not *who* but part of the *what*.

Many news stories are not that simple, though. For example, look at this lead: "The most detailed picture yet made of the center of our Milky Way galaxy may have given scientists their first good glimpse of matter falling into a black hole, two astronomers [*who*] say [*what*]." There is no *where* or *when* in that lead; the point of the lead is simply that two astronomers are saying something.

Clearly, identifying the 4 W's is not a simple matter of underlining subjects and objects or nouns, verbs, and adverbs; it requires that students understand what they are reading in a comprehensive way.

Bonus! The first paragraph of a news story is called the LEAD, pronounced *leed*.

The Big Ideas   page 29

Typically, the main idea of a sports story or a front page news story (steps 1 and 2) will be captured in the headline. Students can check a headline against the *lead*, or the first paragraph of the story, to see if both are emphasizing the same idea.

Editorial content (steps 3 and 4) is quite different. The editorial cartoon and the editorial's main ideas may be more subtle and subjective. In both instances, students may be tempted to stop at a simple idea that, while it is *involved*, does not express *all* of the main idea. Help them express the main editorial ideas in their entirety.

Bonus! Probably *c* is the best answer, though there may be some truth to *a* and *b* as well.

Simply Say It!   page 30

This activity probably works best if the students who write the headlines are not the same ones who separated the original head from the story. You might divide students into groups, providing a variety of newspapers from which they can select short, high-interest stories. Each group would then separate the headlines, mount both the story and its head on colored construction paper, and number the sets on the back so they can be paired later. Groups can then exchange their sets and work either to find the matching parts or to write a headline for each story and then compare it with the original.

Remind students that the headline form should be a "clipped" sentence. Articles are omitted to save space for key words—much the way a telegram or classified ad might be written.

Bonus! "Titanic" is the answer. Encourage students to try writing similar headlines for the activity above, using *only* subjects and verbs.

Once Upon a Time . . .   page 31

Stories that tell how things happened over a period of time are usually not obvious because the first paragraph may give the end result rather than the starting point. In order to complete step 2 of the activity, students must sort out the sequence and, perhaps, use some imagination to explain what happened from start to finish.

Bonus! The four W's are *who*, *what*, *where*, and *when*. Sometimes people add *why* and *how*.

Comprehension Clues   page 32

Usually much more is known about accidents than about crimes. Agatha Christie is said to have taken many of her mystery plots from news stories. Students can have some fun with this activity, trying to imagine the motives, circumstances, fears, and faults of the characters involved. The ability to *infer* such ideas from the facts given involves both creative thinking and problem solving.

Bonus! Rumors usually include a little of both, but lean perhaps more toward inferences than actual facts.

Writing for a Reason   page 33

Editorial content in the newspaper can be fairly complex. An editorial may deal with a variety of issues related to a topic; a letter may deal with a variety of issues and never really seem to get to the subject. Likewise, an editorial piece may seem to accomplish more than one purpose. If the topic and purpose of a piece cannot be identified easily and with clarity, either the reader is not comprehending or the writer is not communicating effectively. Multiple topics and purposes are not a problem unless the reader is confused or mislead by them.

Bonus! Answers will vary according to student tastes. Dramatic books, whether fictional or true-life adventures, are probably the most difficult to put down once you've started reading them.

Facts and Opinions   page 34

Distinguishing fact from opinion is a difficult activity that may require much in-class discussion; it is *not* an activity to be treated as a test! Every good piece of editorial writing will contain fact as well as opinion. Usually fact and opinion will be woven together, making it difficult to distinguish between them.

Here is an example for class discussion. These sentences are taken from a letter to the editor: "Each day my despair for the people on earth and particularly my seven grandchildren increases. Why does mankind continue to war?" The writer expresses the first sentence as a fact. He is telling us for a fact that his despair increases. His question is based on fact, as well. At the time this appeared in the paper, there were a number of hot spots around the world where troops were in combat. *Implied* in both of the writer's sentences is a feeling that he *wishes* the facts were different. But, in fact, the sentences are perfectly factual. Later in the letter, the writer states an opinion: "Today our lives seem to be controlled by political action." That statement is based on his perceptions and feelings. Even though it also may have factual background, it is actually an opinion.

In step 3, the answer to all four statements may be *either* true or false; it all depends on how the writer controls the language.

Bonus! Can the statement be *proven* true or false? What kind of evidence would be needed for proof? This controversial opinion may spark some heated debate in your class. Encourage students to distinguish between fact and opinion in their own statements.

One Person's Opinion   page 35

This activity works especially well with a small group of advanced readers. Students might want to develop their responses to each category individually to begin the activity, but ultimately they should share ideas on the same editorial item in order to glean the greatest amount of meaning from the reading. The activity requires higher-level thinking skills and will work best if the editorial piece has high interest or involves a controversy that stimulates debate among students.

Bonus! An informed opinion is one that is based on reliable, factual information. Editorial writers for the newspaper are avid readers who depend on a wide variety of documented sources to guide their opinions. (The same is not always true of people who write letters to the editor.)

Viewpoints   page 36

Depending on the level and abilities of your students, this activity can lead to a variety of outcomes. Intermediate students might select general topics like animals, accidents, or crime. Older students might pick a more specific event, such as war in the Middle East, or look at connections between events. The idea that everything is connected to something else should be brought out—if not by the students, then by you.

Step 4 of the activity suggests that any given event or issue has substories. Take for example the story "Arson blaze injures 32 in crowded hotel." Substories, as brought out by different points of view, could result in new developments to the arson story. For example, the story says that the hotel was crowded by guests of the Banjo International Convention, but does not say whether the convention was just beginning or just ending. The effects of the fire on that group, and their reactions to how the situation was handled by the hotel, could affect public relations as well as create lawsuits.

The story further reveals that a sequestered jury hearing a political corruption trial was staying in the hotel. The fact that the jury had to be evacuated and relocated could affect the outcome of the trial.

Then there is the viewpoint of the off-duty policeman who found two people, now in critical condition, who were pressed against a door, making it difficult for him to pull them to safety. And there are the viewpoints of the arsonist, the motel manager, the guests, the firemen. The story of this event, though told in the past tense, still has a future that will be shaped by the viewpoints and actions of those involved.

Bonus! There is no limit to what can be written about a strawberry—or any other topic. It is impossible to say ALL about anything!

For some creative thinking, see how many different types of newspaper items about strawberries the class can come up with. For example: stories about crop failure due to weather, development of new hybrids, interview with a farmer, editorial about conditions for strawberry pickers, grocery ads, recipes in the food section, comics involving strawberries, health columns about strawberry allergies, and so on.

Two Sides to Every Story — page 37

To determine viewpoint, students must determine whose thoughts and feelings are represented in the writing. In a crime story, for example, the victim's story is more often reported than the assailant's. Often newspapers will contact a person who is being criticized in a story or column by another person, making an attempt to present both viewpoints, but that is not always possible. When a newspaper story is able to present more than one viewpoint, preferably opposing viewpoints, it is said to be reported *objectively*.

Bonus! Purposely looking at an event from all sides allows us to know and understand the whole idea better. It may cause us to see something we might not *want* to see but *need* to see if we are to really understand what is happening.

Read and React — page 38

This activity will be especially interesting if every student has the same paper. Students will discover that what interests one reader may not attract the attention of another. As students share their reasons why one story, ad, or picture attracted them, they will learn about *each other* while at the same time learning about the paper's content and the details of specific news items.

Pursuing one item of particular interest (step 3) may lead students to send actual letters to the editor—which may even be published. When students read deeply into an article or an issue covered by several articles, they seem to gain confidence as their information grows. Gradually they become more willing to risk stating their opinions—now *informed* opinions—in writing.

Bonus! The best answer is *d*: all of the above. Discuss the fact that bias comes into play with readers as well as writers.

I'm Against It — page 39

Interestingly, people are more likely to write in opposition to something than in support of something, so letters or editorials intended to discourage support are usually not hard to find. Important to the success of this activity is the reader's ability to think of information that might be included but isn't. Encourage students to think of some times when *they* left out certain information on purpose, as, for example, when they wanted to convince or persuade a parent of something.

Bonus! Healthy criticism doesn't tear something down without suggesting a plan for ways to build it back better.

Dear Editor . . . — page 40

The risk in this activity is that students must work with *all* the letters, even those they find uninteresting or complicated. Working in teams or triads will be helpful for students who lack the background or knowledge to fully understand the writers' views.

Bonus! The editor's name usually appears somewhere in the editorial section. Go the next step beyond finding his or her name and extend an invitation for the editor to visit and speak to your class of readers.

Agree—Disagree — page 41

Topics of letters to the editor may not be easy to identify without a cursory reading of each one, which means that steps 1 and 2 could be done almost simultaneously. What is missing between steps 1 and 2 is identifying the position of the writer in relation to the topic. For example, two letters may be addressing the topic of abortion. One is against abortion; the other suggests that there are other forms of killing going on just as serious (if not more serious) than abortion; for example, starving children, increased military buildup, support of a government that sends death squads to kill protesting citizens, and so forth. You may want to spend class time identifying topics and positions in order to facilitate the selection of letters appropriate to students' interests and opinions.

The isolation of key sentences in two of the letters (steps 3 and 4) is a valuable exercise for studying diction, tone, style, and imagery. Usually, in matters of opinion, we react most strongly to emotive language—words that carry feelings and attitudes in addition to their literal meaning.

Teaching Notes: Reading Comprehension   T-9

Bonus! A forum is a public place for open discussion. The letters-to-the-editor section of the newspaper provides a forum for readers.

"Beauty" page 42

The point of this activity is that "meaning" is the connection we make individually between words and images outside us and memories, experiences, and feelings inside us. Step 3 of the activity may be used as a starting point for discussion of what happens when we read something but fail to understand or appreciate the writer's meaning because we have different values.

For example, a headline reads, "Man's (future) best friend." The story tells about a personal robot that looks like an overturned wastebasket on wheels. "It can pick up small objects in its gripper and can move around a room, avoiding people, furniture and walls." And that's about all it can do. It hardly seems like a replacement for "Man's (old) best friend," the faithful dog. But to the researchers, engineers, and high-tech industrialists, it is a science-fiction vision come true. Its beauty and its value are *relative*—as are hundreds of other ideas or objects to which individuals and groups become attached.

Bonus! John Keats wrote: "'Beauty is truth, truth beauty'—that is all/Ye know on earth, and all ye need to know." People operate their lives on what they believe to be true—that which has meaning and value for them. The robot (above) represents "truth and beauty" to the inventor, the designer, and the buyer. There is something intrinsic in its existence that *proves* something. Try to relate the Keats quotation to whatever stories students find in this activity.

Setting page 43

As students work through this activity, they will gain insight into some of the elements of literature that influence meaning and add depth to a story. The activity can be extended by having students actually rewrite one or more of the day's news stories in a new setting. The universality of a news story may become evident as the student discovers that time and place would not change the story's impact, or the drama of the story may become evident as the student discovers that the newsworthiness of an event would have been different if children had not been involved.

Bonus! Obviously answers will differ from student to student. If there are students who think their lives would not be any different, perhaps you need to go through the activity again . . .

Static & Dynamic Characters page 44

Part of what makes comic strips popular is that the characters' static personalities reflect common faults and weaknesses in people. Dagwood's ability to control Blondie's spending will not change—nor will his energy level at work. Charlie Brown will always struggle to succeed. In more serious strips such as Rex Morgan or Judge Parker, people do change as they are influenced by the heroes of the strip.

Extend the discussion beyond the comics to "characters" (people) who appear elsewhere in the paper. Students may note character types among the people involved in front-page news stories that are similar to those of people appearing in the books they have read.

Bonus! Flat characters have a single outstanding characteristic (often a flaw) and always act the same way, whereas round characters are more complex and less predictable.

The Beginning and Ending page 45

The idea that nothing happens in isolation should be emphasized in this activity. A complex network of variables are often involved in a news event. News emerges day by day, week by week. It may be difficult to pinpoint the day a news event began or to imagine that it will ever be "all over." In its largest sense, then, the front page story in today's paper is but a small piece of a greater story—the story of how the world works and how the human race works. Still, its characters and setting and plot can be arranged in short story form, and we can draw meaning from the incidents and interaction of those smaller parts.

Bonus! News usually develops over a period of time. If we miss reading the newspaper for one or two days, or only read it now and then, we may miss one or more key developments in an ongoing story.

Presuming & Predicting page 46

In any good story, the author provides an element of suspense that causes the reader to make mental predictions as the story goes along. We keep reading to see if our predictions are accurate. Curiosity, suspense, and unresolved conflict are all part of what makes people want to read the news every day. In fact, if there are no questions we want to have answered, we may not find reading very exciting.

News stories are filled, either directly or indirectly, with clues about future events. If your classroom provides a safe climate for making predictions and checking assumptions, students are likely to become increasingly curious and interested in finding out if what they thought would happen really happened—thus increasing their knowledge and comprehension of the world around them.

Bonus! Intuition is quick and ready insight, a natural knowing or understanding. It might also be considered "a good guess."

Suspense! page 47

Suppose that the suspenseful story the students find is about a criminal trial, or a war going on in South America, or some new legislation introduced to Congress. Each of these has some of the classic characteristics of a "whodunit." Although the suspect in the criminal case appears guilty, motive is still unknown. The war in South America may not intrigue us much until we discover how directly the United States is involved. Until we decide to write to our congressperson and voice our opinions about the new legislation, we may not care much about what happens with it. When students' curiosity is aroused and their feelings are involved in outcomes, they will take the action necessary to find answers to their questions and pursue their goals.

Bonus! Sherlock Holmes. Point for discussion: In what way is being a good detective involved in citizenship and social responsibility?

To Be Continued . . . page 48

If your students are like most adult readers, they may find that the most interesting story is not an especially pleasant one. We are attracted to the dramatic and to the emotional involvement of drama. The story of the child molested—or the spouse murdered—or the fatal accident—may arouse questions in the reader's mind, questions that reflect genuine fears and feelings. Newspaper exposure to such disturbing real events seems worse to some people than exposure to simulated events of the same sort on television. Classroom experience suggests that students want and need an opportunity to discuss their fears and feelings about the disturbing things they see and hear. In the context of real events, they can handle such serious discussion and learn from each other.

Bonus! No, it is not possible to tell "all" about an event—certainly not in a single news story. "All" would include every conceivable element and full detail, without one aspect or impression left out. That's one reason we continue to read stories about the same event from day to day—to learn more and more as new facts or impressions come to light.

Written Composition

Sentencing! page 49

The primary skill involved in this activity is the ability to recognize the subject and predicate parts of a sentence. As students identify the parts of each headline, mount them on small pieces of construction paper, laminate them with clear contact paper, and put corresponding numbers on the back of each part. Students can use these cards for matching games or sentence-making games.

When students try step 3 of the activity, help them paraphrase the general ideas of each headline rather than use the words of the existing headline.

This activity shows how the newspaper can be used to teach language skills *and* news content simultaneously. As students analyze and rewrite the subjects and verbs of headlines, they must pay attention to the news being discussed by the article.

Bonus! Subject-verb sentences are not hard to write, and as students gain confidence, their sentences will reflect their sophistication. Point for discussion: Students may try writing commands, like "Go away." This is a complete sentence using only two words, but the two words are *not* subject and verb; the subject (you) is understood. Does that make it, technically, a three-word sentence?

Playing with Words page 50

Fluency and freedom with language develop as students learn that language is flexible and that they can manipulate it. Part of the fun of this activity is for students to see how much meaning they can pack into one word, or how they can control and change meaning by the way they arrange words in a certain format or sequence. Steps 1 and 2 require the use of subjects and verbs only. Step 3 frees the writer to use any two-word combination.

A student once used this activity to review a story that appeared in the paper just a week or so before the May eruption of Mount St. Helens in 1980. Here is what he wrote: "Steam billows. Ash pours. Gases heat. Lava rises? Eruption nears? Geologists watch. History waits."

Bonus! The story is "Jack and Jill," with a little extra interpretation.

Sensitivity   page 51

This activity continues to develop the skills of fluency and control in composition. As students list things they *see* in the picture (step 1), their list will consist primarily of nouns (*house, man*). In step 2, when they write another word *after* the naming word, chances are it will be a verb (house *burns*; man *runs*). However, some students may write combinations like "fire hot" or "man afraid." Combinations like these provide excellent material to use with the entire group to demonstrate the process of selecting and refining word choice: What is a verb that conveys "hot" in connection with fire? What is a more specific word that conveys "hot fire"? Through this kind of questioning, students may arrive at a stronger statement, such as "flames scorch" or "occupant flees."

Bonus! Awareness is probably more important. Sometimes we can concentrate too hard and miss the very thing we are looking for. Awareness, on the other hand, suggests that our "feelers" are sensitive to all kinds of stimuli at once.

Sentence Combining   page 52

For best results, you should do step 1 yourself the first time and have your students do steps 2 and 3 as a whole group. Once they understand the process, students can work in pairs to select the article and compose the short, kernel sentences. Pairs then exchange their sets of sentences for completion of steps 2 and 3. Try to provide students with a variety of newspapers or, at least, a variety of news stories.

Bonus! Although there are other options, the obvious solution is "Mary had a little lamb."

A Funny
Thing Happened . . .   page 53

This activity provides an opportunity for students to practice writing narrative and dialogue. Since the story is already clear, their task is to accurately and effectively rewrite the picture-version in words. Students will likely know what they want to say, but will struggle with the right way to say it. They will know how the characters interact, but will struggle with finding language forms and conventions that capture the essence of the story and its humor.

Bonus! The answer probably depends on whether or not the written version is done in handwriting or is typeset. Students can determine about how much space their written explanations would take by counting the number of words they wrote, then counting out an equal number of words in a column of regular type. Compare: Is that more or less space than the cartoon itself takes?

Paragraphs—
Easy as ABC   page 54

Here's a simple formula for writing a paragraph to state a preference, supported by detail or rationale. While this formula models tight reasoning and controlled writing, it is not meant to suggest that *all* paragraphs work this way. After students have tried using the model on three or four news articles (the most interesting, the most tragic, the most humorous, the most educational, and so forth), move to the editorial page. Ask students to see if they can find a consistent organizational pattern for paragraphs in the editorials or letters to the editor.

Bonus! Almost beyond comprehension! Don't even figure getting half! It just kinda leaves most normal, ordinary people quietly ruminating, scribbling, testing ubiquitous verbosity while Xeroxing yawning zeros . . .

No Two Alike!   page 55

The purpose here is to help students discover something they will be willing to write about. Their attitudes toward people—their mental and physical capabilities, their beliefs and values, their personal appearance and lifestyle—will emerge as students study real-life examples. Until we discover what we feel or believe about a topic, we have no particular reason to write about it. This activity can provide the structure by which students sharpen their knowledge and convictions about individuality, equality, fairness, human rights, and personal standards.

Bonus! Each of the letters shown will probably have at least one fan, and all three will be liked for different reasons.

Making Sense — page 56

How to organize information is an important decision in the writing process. The reader must be able to follow the writer's lead in order to fully comprehend the message.

The articles chosen for this activity should be both interesting and important, if possible. If they are straight news stories, they will most likely follow the inverted pyramid style: the most important information first, followed by less important supporting details. A feature story may follow a time sequence; an editorial may use cause-effect organization; an in-depth analysis may use comparison/contrast. To discover the organization of a piece of writing, students can try to outline it or to "map" it, showing relationships between the topics and ideas expressed in the writing.

Bonus! A fair would more likely be described by layout or design (spatial sequence) than either a ball game or a speech.

Read On! Read On! — page 57

Students are asked to study the introduction and conclusion of a feature story. Unlike the typical news story, most feature stories use a form of suspended interest to keep the reader's attention. Step 2 of the activity asks the student to identify questions or unresolved conflicts that demand further explanation (and reading). In conjunction with step 4, ask students to describe the best book they've ever read, or ask them why they are anxious to read a note someone has passed to them. What do they want the book or note to *say* to them, *do* for them, *mean* to them? Finally, what did the writer of the feature story achieve?

Bonus! *Tale of Two Cities* begins with that line. It is describing the time of the French revolution. Point for discussion: Could those phrases be used to describe *any* era in history? Why or why not? Why is it a good introduction to a story?

Create-a-Character — page 58

This activity encourages creativity and imaginative thinking. Unfamiliar faces from the news will probably work better than familiar ones. The process of devising relationships based on real pictures may help students discover or develop a plot. By creating the characters, putting words in their mouths, and building their relationships, a whole story may emerge. Even if it doesn't, students will at least begin to sense the power that characters have in *causing* the events of a narrative.

Bonus! Agatha Christie probably used all of these for inspiration, but it is said that she especially used the newspaper as a source for characters and conflicts.

Fact & Fiction — page 59

Encourage students to be completely open to new ideas in order to develop a totally new story based on the picture they choose. Suggest that they put the pictured events into a new place and a new time, if that helps. Students can develop conflict by suggesting to their readers that an unsolvable problem exists. The point of their story, then, is to tell how the problem or conflict was solved.

Bonus! Generally, we read to see how a *conflict* will be resolved. But, of course, *characters* and *climax* are both important and interesting elements in the resolution of conflict.

Fact & Fantasy — page 60

Encourage students to be more explicit in describing their film preferences than simply writing "because I saw it before and I liked it" or "because I don't like it." Challenge them to identify three or four *specific reasons* for their choices.

In step 3, discuss believability in stories. People are said to watch TV drama because they enjoy the vicarious experience it provides. We often enjoy stories that seem believable (factual), but we also enjoy imagining what we have never seen or experienced (fantasy). Which of those elements exists in the two films each student selected?

Bonus! "*Truth* is stranger than fiction." Point for discussion: Is there a story in today's paper that would seem like fantasy if it were made into a movie?

Rhyme & Reason — page 61

This activity can offer an outlet for students' feelings and frustrations about situations in the world that seem uncontrolled and uncontrollable. As they express their feelings, they may hit upon ideas for involving themselves in solutions. At the very least, the activity can help clarify for the writer how important the event or issue is, and who is responsible for taking action. Again, an activity like this provides a way for skill and substance to meet in a meaningful learning experience. As students capture in words their feelings about current events, their knowledge of and attitudes toward those events will be clarified.

Bonus! Poetry done in picture form is called *concrete poetry*. The words are written or typeset to create visual images, the way the repeated word *hills* does in the cartoon.

The Heart of the Matter page 62

The challenge of putting ourselves in another's shoes can help us better understand the drama and emotion of a situation. By putting an exact moment into play form, the elements of drama will become clear: who the characters are and what makes them respond as they do; how setting contributes to the scene; what constitutes the core of the conflict that is producing the emotion. This activity will have added impact when students realize they are replaying a scene from real life.

Bonus! *Empathy* is the preferred answer; readers should feel just as the real characters themselves felt. Point for discussion: how does *sympathy* differ from *empathy*?

Good Senses page 63

To capture on paper the sights, sounds, feelings, and tastes of a slice of life requires careful attention to detail and a sensitive imagination. Writing in teams of two may enhance this activity as students help each other say what they sense. Tragic accidents or crimes are likely to become the focus of this activity unless students are encouraged to explore other kinds of news content, such as recipes, sports reports, weather news, or feature stories. Allow students the freedom to explore any aspect of a story, as long as they can defend the connection between what they are describing in great detail and the event itself.

Bonus! E.S.P. stands for *extra-sensory perception*. It refers to the apparent ability of some people to know things through intuition or an extra sense beyond the five senses normal people have.

The Five Senses page 64

Although it is possible that a single picture could represent all five of the senses, encourage students to select five different pictures. Allow students to help each other discover words or phrases that will best convey the sensory detail required. In writing the descriptions, students might take a variety of viewpoints: a child grimacing at the taste of pickled beets vs. an adult savoring it; the sound of the alarm clock on the first day of hunting season vs. the sound of the alarm at 6:30 A.M. on a Monday morning.

Bonus! The sixth sense is our ability to know something through intuition or E.S.P.

Faces with Feelings page 65

Photographs are preferred over cartoon drawings for this activity because they will reinforce the reality of emotion in real-life drama, but either can be used effectively. As students begin to describe what they think is causing the emotion in each case, they may insist that a person or a situation is causing the emotion. Suggest that two people experiencing the same situation might react quite differently. Therefore: are emotions caused by external circumstances, or are they caused by internal responses to external circumstances? If students are able to pursue this line of thinking, they may get helpful insights into people and relationships.

Bonus! Artists usually emphasize emotion through the eyes, although the mouth is more important in very simple drawings like smiley-faces or frown-faces. Often, eyes and mouth together suggest a particular emotion.

From Start to Finish page 66

This activity focuses on the importance and process of prewriting. Before students can write what they want to say, they must gather some possibilities. In step 1 they begin to identify possible emotions. In step 2 they list as much sensory detail as they can imagine. It isn't until step 3 that they begin to articulate the relationship between the emotion and the stimuli and try to say what might have been happening for the person involved. What students write about in step 3 will be stronger when they have spent the time thinking about steps 1 and 2.

Bonus! Writing down all a character's thoughts is called "stream of consciousness." Most of the time we are not aware of the full range of our thoughts or the reasons for them. Putting them *all* down on paper can reveal things we never realized about ourselves.

Lost & Found page 67

Students can have a lot of fun with this activity as they take real-life circumstances and build fantasies around them. The conflict or plot is already suggested by the dilemma that prompted someone to place the ad in the paper. Now students must create the characters, the setting, and the dynamics to heighten the drama and resolve the conflict. The student's point of view is likely to be that of the person who wrote the ad, but it might also be that of the person who holds the answer to the ad.

Bonus! Antonyms (opposites). Ask students to give examples of the other *-nym* words. (Zaponym is a nonsense word; students might be very creative in finding examples for it!)

You Are There   page 68

The prewriting technique of gathering and listing potential story elements is important to the development of a strong, descriptive account. The activity directions do not address the organization of this information; you might want to discuss different possibilities before students begin step 4. Often dramatic events are reported in time sequence. However, step 3 suggests that the writer might take a position about the rightness or wrongness of what happened, and that might call for a cause/effect organization or a form of persuasive argument, where the writer states a position and supports it with a logical rationale.

Bonus! A piece of writing that tells a story is called *narrative*.

You're Kidding   page 69

Newspapers may not offer a wide variety of articles to choose from for this activity, nor will they be easy for students to identify. An editorial cartoon or social-political comic strip may be a good place to begin. Follow up with display advertisements or humorous news stories. Finally, have students study columnists whose writing is intended to point up human weaknesses and inconsistencies. Questions such as "Is this a war movie or am I watching the news?" and "Who will test those who are designing the tests for teachers?" carry messages deeper than the questions themselves and are meant to be more serious than they appear. The activity provides an in-depth analysis of language control.

Bonus! *Satire* is the use of wit, irony, sarcasm, and exaggeration to make fun of human weaknesses.

Whadja Say??   page 70

The newspaper usually models correct forms of written language. Probably the best examples of less formal language will be found on the comic page, where characters engage in casual conversation. Even in the comics, though, students should be able to detect the difference between the speech patterns of "professional" and "common" characters.

As an extension to the activity, tape a student *telling* about a front page story; then tape a student reading the same story. Points for discussion: How is spoken language different from written language? Would the newspaper be harder or easier to read if we tried to write the news in conversational language?

Bonus! "Whadja say?" translates to "What did you say?"

Mixed Up   page 71

In order to do this activity, students will have to pay close attention to word clues, logic, and sequence. The final story will be largely incoherent, but it should hang together to the extent that all the words sound like they belong. Illustrate the idea of the activity by showing how the subject of one headline ("Supreme Court . . . ") fits with the predicate of another headline (" . . . seeks release."). Fitting lines or paragraphs of news stories together will take some doing, but it will challenge students to pay attention to language patterns and sequence of thought.

Bonus! If a piece of writing has coherence, it has order and logic. An incoherent piece of writing is disorganized and makes no sense.

Literary Themes

Struggle   page 72

This activity not only helps students identify the four types of conflict, it also offers them models of how people deal with conflict. Typically, people view conflict as a negative factor in life, yet almost every person who is greatly admired by others has won that recognition by overcoming conflict. Of the four types of conflict, "man against self" may be the most difficult to identify in the newspaper. Help students locate and interpret news stories in which the person involved is likely to suffer self-doubt, guilt, emotional pain, or fear as a result of the event; for example, the driver of a school bus that went off an icy road and over an embankment, resulting in the death of two passengers.

Bonus! Some discussion before students write may result in some excellent essays or personal narratives.

Struggle and Strife   page 73

The characters involved in a conflict are often easier to identify than the lessons to be learned. The two following front-page stories are typical of what students may find: (1) a story about the bad weather and the strife it is causing, through no one's fault; (2) a story of two planes colliding because one went down the wrong runway in heavy fog. The values and qualities to be learned from these stories of strife range from finding the patience to deal with what we cannot change (weather), to granting forgiveness for other's mistakes or ignorance, which have caused us loss or injury. All of us will encounter similar problems in our lifetime. It can be easier to learn values like patience and forgiveness from a situation in which we are not directly and emotionally involved.

Bonus! From this experience, students may recognize that it is *conflict* that makes our lives interesting.

Mishaps and Other Misfortunes   page 74

In this activity students look for stories in which someone experiences personal loss, pain, or injury. There may be safety lessons to be learned, or there may be lessons about acceptance and about going on in spite of the past.

Fiction is built out of just this kind of material. If students can learn to glean lessons for themselves and others while reading about real-life experiences in the news, it should be easier for them to find similar themes and make similar generalizations when reading literature.

Bonus! "He is truly wise who gains wisdom from another's mishap."

Choosing Our Responses   page 75

How people handle themselves at critical times in their lives is the focus of this activity. Listing specific details of what people do and say in response to crisis may require some inference, close reading, or both. It will probably be easier for students to locate and identify responses to *bad* news than to good. For example, it is usually reported quite matter-of-factly that a person once thought to be missing has now turned up. As readers, we can only imagine how his family must have responded upon hearing of his whereabouts. Similarly, the announcement of a person's being promoted or hired for a new position rarely includes any of the personal response that must have been expressed when the event actually occurred.

Bonus! Rudyard Kipling, in the poem "If."

Good Ones & Bad Ones   page 76

This activity looks at the motives and morals of people whose acts, good or bad, have made news. Once in a while a news story will give some background information about a character involved in the story, suggesting possible influences in that person's life that could have motivated the action. This type of reporting, however, is rare. In this activity, the students must draw on several resources—their personal experience, the details of the story, and their creative imagination—to put together reasons and motives for what happened. This is the same kind of interpretive reading students must do for poetry or fiction. The only difference is that in real-life situations, the writer is merely reporting facts as they appear to be at the time; whereas in fiction, the writer presents facts with the expectation that the reader will draw certain inferences from them.

Bonus! Self-image—our opinion of ourselves, who we think we are—is usually involved in the actions we take, and was probably involved in the news stories in some way. Point for discussion: What is the self-image of someone who does something labeled "bad" by others?

Change of a Lifetime   page 77

Life-changing events can vary considerably in degree and quality. The event can be as common as a birth or death announcement. What the student chooses to deal with in a short story (step 3) may be a person directly involved in the story *or* someone else affected by that person's actions. Important to the success of the activity will be the student's willingness to pursue the whole range of possible emotional responses, in order to select out of the possibilities those responses that will provide the strongest message in short story form.

Bonus! The Bonus question would make a good journal-writing or essay assignment. There could be additional benefit if students are willing to share what they write, although no one should be forced to do so.

Ups and Downs — page 78

This activity takes advantage of the frequent "personality" features in the news that provide an in-depth study of the events and circumstances that have shaped a person's life. The study of timing and sequence in real-life situations can help you teach the elements of drama and climax in the development of a plot in literature. This structure provides a way for students to think and talk about events that create change in our lives and influence future choices we make. This activity resembles "bibliotherapy" in that it opens topics for discussion in a non-threatening way.

Bonus! Suggest that students consider making only partial lifelines—from 0 to 50 years—so that they will have enough space to include all of what they consider *major* events. Help them see how much of their lives is still out there to be lived. Point for discussion: How much should they allow an event during the first twelve to fifteen years influence all the rest of their life?

Turning Points — page 79

Accidents, choices, planned events, or opportunities may all be cited in this activity as turning points in a person's life. Locating the ages of the people involved on the time line might help students realize that they themselves are closer in age to some life-changing possibilities than they may think.

Another value in this activity comes with reflecting on the fact that all kinds of things, good and bad, may happen to change our lives. If such events are unplanned and completely unanticipated, we may be caught off-guard and respond less reasonably than if we had thought out a response before the fact.

Bonus! Sometimes students think that nothing ever happens to them. Point for discussion: How much control do we have over the direction our life is taking? Can we *create* turning points?

Meanness vs. Courage — page 80

It has been said that the newspaper is the best record we have of the magnificent courage and the incredible meanness of the human race. There will be examples of each quality in a daily newspaper, for almost every case of meanness prompts someone else to act courageously. More interesting to consider than the act itself, however, are the motivations and the consequences of the act.

A person acts with meanness or with courage in response to a specific situation, either as attacker, victim, or rescuer. Anger can motivate either meanness or courage, depending on the circumstances—and the desired consequences. This activity focuses student attention on strong emotions, the actions provoked by such emotions, and the results of those actions.

Bonus! "Never start a fight, but always be prepared to save a life" would be one way to paraphrase the quotation. Generally, it is advice to go through life peacefully, without hostility ("speak softly"), yet always prepared for a crisis, knowing you have the strength ("a big stick") to react forcefully if necessary.

He-roes and Her-oes — page 81

This activity may lead to some interesting insights about what it means to be heroic. Students are asked to look for examples of ability, strength, and courage. They may find those qualities in athletes; in local, national, or world leaders; or in people victimized by circumstances.

Step 3 of the activity invites the student to make a connection between people in the news and personal experience. The intent is that students will come to see themselves as performing with great ability, strength, and courage—whether in the past, present, or future.

Bonus! Luck, taken alone, is usually not a factor in deeds of heroism.

Heroic Action — page 82

The student who follows each step of this activity will ultimately deal with values and motives. The "hero," in writing a journal entry (step 4), will be expressing feelings and reliving the experience, but must explain also the flow of thoughts that accompanied his or her action. It is possible that the student will observe a weakness in a character of a news story and choose to deal with that person's responses to the event as well.

The astute reader and writer will find in this activity the opportunity to develop an entire network of reasons and responses, portraying the complexity of human decision-making at a point of crisis.

Bonus! An unsung hero is one who does not get the recognition deserved.

Help for the Hapless — page 83

All kinds of public or community services may be considered in this activity. Sometimes people write letters to the editor in which they praise or thank someone. It is enlightening to see how much or how little recognition there is for all the help people give one another in a day or a week.

In step 3 students will be looking for "victims" in need of help. They may be surprised to discover that they have more power than they think to offer help to people in need. The activity offers an opportunity for students to think about the role they might play in serving the needs of other people.

Bonus! A newspaper offers ads with discount coupons for food for the poor, announcements of special events and groups for the lonely, and medical columns with advice for the ill.

Desire and Determination   page 84

Sports stories provide consistent examples of self-discipline and attitude control. Careful study of famous athletes will show that their abilities do not "come naturally." Students can find on almost any sports page an athlete who has played in spite of a sore shoulder, a stiff knee, or a case of flu. They will find players who have been benched and must accept that disappointment, yet who still play with enthusiasm and emotion during the short period of time they are called in to relieve a regular player. They will find players who admit they made mistakes or who were in some way poorly prepared for the competition. They will encounter players who *know* they are good and give credit to the coach, the other team members, or someone else who helped them be good.

Once the activity is completed, arrange to spend some time discussing what students have discovered. If a variety of newspapers are used, students may want to share what they learned about different athletes. As an extension to the activity, help students make a connection between the physical training and discipline needed for outstanding sports performances and the intellectual training and discipline demanded for excellent academic performances.

Bonus! A specific goal is probably the key to success, since it can inspire a person to do *whatever is needed* to achieve that goal (including the practice of self-discipline).

Good Sports   page 85

By analyzing the comments made by and about the winners and losers in sports events, students may learn something about the power of attitudes. The phenomenon of losing is especially interesting because it is something everyone fears yet all must experience at one time or another. Both coaches and players admit to being less than their best in times of failure; usually they will praise their opponents' skill and, as one coach put it, their "moxie."

As an extension to this activity, suggest that students look for lessons about winning and losing in the "game of life." Who or what are "the opponents"?

Bonus! Losers need positive advice, suggestions about how and what to change, rather than reminders of what they did that was wrong.

Success   page 86

Students work on the ability to extrapolate information and meaning from news items in this activity. For example, was the mayor successful in getting what he wanted when he won the election by only a small margin? Were the astronauts successful when they landed safely, despite a variety of small failures on their spacecraft? What was their major goal—to land safely, to be astronauts, to have a flawless mission?

In step 2 the student is asked to name other people who were involved with the accomplishment. Almost always one person's success depends on the support of others.

This activity works especially well for teams of at least two students because the exploration of ideas is more important than arriving at any particular "right" answer.

Bonus! *Desire* is another key to success; we must really want something in order to create the energy and drive to go after it.

What Families Are For   page 87

Although a special feature story is more likely to include something about each member of a family, news stories about families are not uncommon. Often, such a story will indicate special relationships within the family structure. A columnist in one paper speaks of losing a mother-in-law to cancer and describes the important role that the woman's children play in helping her die. Another story describes a young couple and their fight to save the life of their second child, an eight-month-old boy who is severely handicapped. One important discovery that can come while doing this activity (step 2) is learning that every family member is important in different ways.

Bonus! Students may enjoy clipping words from the newspaper to make their acrostic.

Personal Profiles — page 88

Newspaper features about people appear often, exhibiting the same qualities and making the same contributions as full-length biographies. Learning about what makes people the way they are can be invaluable to students as they are forming their own personal values. This activity works especially well if you prepare in advance by clipping appropriate stories over a period of several days or weeks so that the students are able to study different people.

Students can create "poster profiles" of each personality, using the person's picture in combination with adjectives and quotations extracted from the articles. Students might share their profiles and vote to decide which person would be most interesting to invite to the classroom as a special guest. And if the person is local—do it!

Bonus! Personality, which is revealed through our behavior and attitudes, may not always match character qualities, which are sometimes concealed. Usually, though, a person's character is reflected in some part of his or her personality.

Virtues of a Valentine — page 89

The qualities that make people lovable are more internal than external. Before doing this activity, ask students to list the six qualities they admire most in other people. Chances are good that they will list qualities like kindness, humor, courage, and humility ahead of good looks, attractive hair, beautiful clothes, and nice cars. Follow with some discussion about the deceptiveness of appearance in the selection of close friends.

This activity can be used at any time to illustrate the qualities that make us inherently lovable, as opposed to the ways we sometimes act to attract attention from the opposite sex.

Bonus! The four cardinal virtues are justice (fairness), prudence (wisdom), fortitude (strength), and temperance (self-control).

Mother's Day — page 90

Although designed for Mother's Day, this activity models a way to give recognition to anyone on any special occasion. It has been used for thank-you cards following a field trip, as well as cards honoring the school secretary during National Secretary Week. One class used this idea to create get-well cards for a student who had an extended hospital stay. It can become an art project as well as a language activity. Encourage students to keep the words as positive as possible. Ads often provide a wide variety of good words to choose from.

Bonus! No one knows for sure where Mother Goose originated, but it has been suggested that the ancient French Queen Goosefoot (Reine Pedance), or Bertha-with-the-great-foot, who was the mother of Charlemagne and known as a great storyteller, might have been the original Mother Goose.

Father's Day — page 91

This activity provides another opportunity for students to produce an art project that expresses values and character qualities. The words and pictures selected should of course be positive. Colored construction paper makes an attractive base for this project.

Bonus! Your paternal grandparents are your *father's* mother and father. Vocabulary extension: what is the word for your *mother's* parents?

The Way I See Me... — page 92

All of us like to believe that someday we will be better than we are today. Students may tend to select some fairly negative words to describe their present, even though they want to be very different (and better) five years from now. The activity can help students begin to formulate ideas and dreams about how they want to be someday, but more importantly, it should help them see that what they are doing now, and the way they see themselves now, is already affecting their future—an idea they can explore in the Bonus activity.

Bonus! This question makes an excellent essay topic.

Free Advice — page 93

Reading about other's problems can sometimes help us understand our own. The activity asks students to identify clearly the problem and feeling about the problem, *as they are stated by the writer*. In doing so, the student may be able to discern attitudes or misperceptions that contribute to the writer's problems.

To prepare for this activity, consider selecting the letters ahead of time and separating each letter from its answer. This procedure will save class time as well as assure content appropriate for the age level and interests of your students. Additionally, students will be interested in seeing how close their answers come to the professional response.

Bonus! No single person can expect to be fully informed on *all* the issues—social, political, economic, environmental—involved in governing our country. The broader our interests and responsibilities are, the wiser we are to seek advice.

Candid Comics   page 94

The most popular comics are those that reflect human weaknesses and foibles. Furthermore, the best-read news articles are those that describe unusual human situations. Both represent exaggerations of what is considered normal.

This activity can lead to further study of humor as a specific literary technique. The ability to see humor in everyday situations is a particularly valuable quality to develop, as long as we do not become callous to the feelings and perceptions of others.

Bonus! Dagwood and Blondie were married in the comics on February 13, 1933.

Laughing Matter   page 95

Humor is often achieved through subtle combinations of situation, word choice, and special techniques. The given list of types of humor may imply that humor is achieved primarily through language, but in fact art, too, can create surprise, incongruity, and distortion. By looking at humor in different types of cartoons, students can get a better sense of what to look for in literary comedy. They can also learn how to better achieve humor in their own writing.

Bonus! Sarcasm belittles and insults people. Wit and satire take advantage of the moment, but are less likely to be hurtful.

Nonverbal Communication

Louder Than Words   page 96

Just as there is power in a well-placed word or a well-turned phrase, there is power in a strategic stroke of a pen or brush. This activity demonstrates how nonverbal elements like color, size, texture, arrangement, facial expression, and clothing styles communicate. Each of these can be used to say things that will affect people in specific ways. Artists can predict how people will respond to certain combinations of elements, just as the skilled writer can predict what words will make people understand the intended message. If an artist fails to provoke any response to the elements of an ad, for example, then that ad is not a success—for it won't sell any merchandise if people don't even read it.

Bonus! All are important, but first and foremost an ad must get the reader's attention.

Lettering   page 97

The intent of this activity is to illustrate how lettering styles are a communicative art form. The formation of letters in unique and consistent ways brings together verbal and nonverbal messages. When students select a lettering style for their own names, they may recognize that their choice reflects how they view themselves.

Bonus! Calligraphy is the art of handwriting.

Line Drawings   page 98

Having done step 1, students will be quicker to recognize the use of straight and curved lines as design elements in advertisements. Help students see how lines are used other than for illustrations and lettering: they frequently separate parts of ads, provide organization to a complex ad, and assist the reader in following a certain pattern or sequence. The heaviness of the lines used also communicates a feeling, and is usually consistent with the lettering style and the illustrations in the same design. The interpretation of nonverbal content in an ad is an important skill to develop, for it can help students understand language at an abstract level.

Bonus! A broken line is used for coupons or other items intended to be clipped and saved.

Creative Creations   page 99

Prepare for this activity by searching yourself for samples of striking graphic design in the newspaper to show students before they begin. Sometimes just a small part of an ad will combine artistic elements to create a special effect. It may be a trademark or a special-effects photo that gets your attention. In step 3, the students are to arrange a graphic message of their own in a collage or montage of clippings from the paper.

Bonus! Graffiti are inscriptions, slogans, or drawings scribbled crudely on walls or in any public place.

Color Added · page 100

This activity illustrates the power of color in advertising. The use of color markers (rather than crayons) with older students, while requiring more precision, will yield more intense colors and a more professional-looking result. Step 3 calls for the students to reproduce half of the ad in a pencil drawing—a test not only of the power of color but of students' visual perception, as well. As an extension of the activity, suggest that one or two students research to find out the cost of a black and white ad vs. costs of adding one, two, and three colors to ads of the same size.

Bonus! Red, blue, and yellow are the basic colors. Invite someone involved in printing production in your community to demonstrate how full-color prints are made using the process called *color separation*.

Warm and Cool Colors · page 101

There are a couple of color theories students may want to test. One suggests that advertisers will use warm colors more often, particularly red, because they catch the reader's attention better. The other theory is that advertisers use colors consistent with their product and with the weather; for example, *blue* for selling air conditioners in the heat of summer, *red* for selling heaters in the dead of winter. With a bit of research, students could turn up very different answers and theories.

For an extension of this activity, suggest that one student call the advertising department at your local paper to find out who chooses the color for ads and how advertisers are advised about which colors to use.

Bonus! Anger is considered warm; jealousy is considered cold.

Sign Language · page 102

One of the earliest forms of written language we learn as small children is that of signs and trademarks. Through judicious use of color, symbols, shapes, and arrangement, even nonreaders can get the printed message.

Step 3 of the activity requires the student to find reference material on the topic of trademarks. Pursue the importance of symbols for communication by asking students to identify international symbols (that is, those that are understood around the world).

Bonus! The MasterCard credit card is represented by overlapping red and gold circles.

Trademarks · page 103

Plan to supply students with a variety of newspapers, including plenty from the days when advertising is heaviest. That way students will be able to find a greater variety of trademarks. You can create identification games or quizzes using the signs and symbols that students find. They may be surprised to discover that without the name or picture of the trademarked item, they will often be unable to recognize the logo—even though they have seen it often.

In designing their own trademarks (step 3), students will want to think about characteristic symbols—something that will tie their name and their best qualities together.

Bonus! The VISA symbol in an ad means that the store will honor that credit card for purchases you make there.

The Art of Persuading · page 104

This activity invites the students to do some problem solving by inventing a new product or service to fill a specific need they perceive. Students may better understand the world of marketing as they create and then try to sell their idea for a product that would make a better world.

In designing their ad (step 3), students should think about how to convince prospective buyers who don't think the new product is needed, who don't believe it will work, who do not understand it, or who think they can make something of their own that will work just as well. They may come to see the importance of marketing when they realize that an ad could determine whether the public would make any effort toward buying what the advertiser has to sell.

Bonus! A Frenchman, Comte Mede de Sivrac, invented the bicycle in 1790.

Looks on Faces — page 105

If students clip most of the faces from ads, they will probably have a bunch of happy faces because advertisers usually portray people who are happy with their product. If the students clip faces from news photos, they may have a more accurate study of the way people really feel much of the time.

For step 3, students should be encouraged to find an article that suggests a variety of emotions, depending on the roles played by different characters in the story. The space provided on the worksheet for step 3 will be inadequate for many students; encourage the use of other paper for a full interpretation of the situation stimulating the various emotions.

Bonus! When our feelings are hurt, we probably feel *embarrassment* first, then *anger*.

Masks — page 106

This makes an especially fitting activity around Halloween or Mardi Gras, but is really appropriate any time of year. If genuine masks are available, use them to demonstrate what the creator has done to eyes, eyebrows, and mouth to emphasize expression.

As an extension, there's an opportunity here for students to play around with psychology, discussing why certain expressions are predictable on certain faces in the newspaper, either in ads or photos; for example, the President's wife smiling, the shoppers in ads pleased and happy, certain cartoon characters always angry or upset.

Bonus! The kind of person behind this "mask" might be expected to be confident, happy, satisfied, prosperous, and not facing any big problems in her life.

Costumes — page 107

This activity focuses on clothing styles as a communicator of age, sex, role, and personality. Illustrations will probably be found most easily in ads, but appropriate news photos will present an even stronger statement about the relationship of dress to activities.

Use the school setting to introduce the idea that everyone wears a "costume." The janitor does, the cooks do, the principal does, teachers do, and students do. The most daring teacher will introduce this activity by wearing to school that day something out of character—just to demonstrate to students that we really do wear "costumes" every day, not just for Halloween or performing plays.

Bonus! Costumes vary greatly, are often very individualistic, and usually are worn to suggest that we are something we are not. Uniforms on the other hand convey sameness and practicality, and often are worn to communicate to people who and what we are.

Characters — page 108

Search newspapers for some examples ahead of time to illustrate what students should be looking for in step 1. The mass media are often criticized for their reinforcement of stereotypes through ads and news content. Stereotypes suggest that people of a certain age, race, sex, religion, or other general group are all the same. Stereotypes can be limiting and harmful because they create expectations that everyone in the group will always exhibit certain behaviors and engage in certain common activities. Male/female roles are probably the most common stereotypes, but students may want to look at *all* kinds of stereotyping, particularly in ads.

Bonus! Ask students to write their answers to this question without letting others see their ideas. It will be interesting to see how much similarity there is in answers they arrived at independently.

Lively Bodies — page 109

The sports pages are probably the best place to find photos of bodies in motion. By drawing stick figures over the athletes, students can begin to discover how artists convey certain body movements.

Cartooning is an art form that appeals to all ages, and students frequently express a desire to animate characters. Step 3 offers that opportunity.

Bonus! ANIMATED ANATOMIES.

Tricks and Techniques — page 110

The simpler the drawings in the cartoons, the easier the analysis will be for students. The placement and attitude of eyes, eyebrows, and mouth usually determine facial expression.

To illustrate different approaches to humor, find and enlarge one sample comic strip in which there is humor without any dialogue, and another in which there is little change in animation but considerable dialogue.

The creation of humor is often subtle. Discuss real-life humor; ask students to recall examples of something that was funny when it happened, but when retold later lost its humor. Why did that happen? Are the lines of comic strips funny when retold without the support of the drawings?

As an extension, ask students to vote on the funniest cartoon on a given day—and the least funny cartoon. Is there agreement? Why or why not?

Bonus! The eyes labeled *A* might be fearful, dejected, or perplexed. The eyes labeled *B* look angry or determined.

Kinds of Cartoons   page 111

The first three types of cartoons should be easy to find in most daily newspapers. It is important that students recognize the differences between cartoons that are designed to entertain and those that are designed to comment on critical issues and events. Humor frequently depends on exaggeration and incongruity. Extremes can often be illustrated more effectively than they can be described. As an extension, challenge students to try *writing* a joke that recreates the humor of a cartoon without the use of pictures.

Bonus! Bill Mauldin won the Pulitzer prize in 1945 and 1959 for his editorial cartoons portraying war.

Details, Details   page 112

Where an artist has repeated a background in two or more frames, how can you prove that the background was not photocopied? How can you prove that each frame was drawn separately? Students may need a magnifying glass and a ruler, but usually they can easily spot the slight differences once they look for them.

As a variation of this activity, ask students to study an ad for two minutes, then turn their papers over and answer five questions about details in the ad: for example, the price of a featured item, the store's hours, the presence or absence of color, a description of the store's symbol, the name of the item in the lower right corner of the ad.

Bonus! The initials AHM appear just above the shadow.

Slight (?!) Exaggerations!   page 113

Depending on the level of your students, you may need to collect appropriate editorial cartoons over a period of time to distribute for use with this activity. If your students are not following the news regularly, some cartoons will be meaningless to them. They will benefit by working in teams to complete this assignment because what one student doesn't know, another might.

The first task in interpreting editorial cartoons is separating real people from symbols. Almost all of the art in an editorial cartoon carries meaning and is, therefore, symbolic. Only after isolating the important elements of the cartoon will the student be ready to capsulize its message (step 4).

Bonus! Both are artists' interpretations of people, but a caricature distorts reality to make a point, while a portrait is more realistic and tries to capture a person's true essence.

Cartoons That Comment   page 114

The editorial cartoon is an extremely valuable teaching tool. The topic is usually timely, significant, and controversial. The editorial cartoon points students back to the front page to learn the facts about whatever is at issue. The cartoonist is skilled at getting to the core of a complex issue. So subtle and so complex are the elements that students need to learn a technique for sifting and sorting through the levels of meaning. Basically, this sifting technique involves answering four questions: Who are the people? What are the symbols? What are the facts? What are the opinions? It is important to ask about the opinion last because that is the most obvious feature—but opinion has no power unless it is first based on fact.

Bonus! Thomas Nast was one of the first editorial cartoonists and was the originator of two famous political symbols, the Democratic donkey and the Republican elephant. He also popularized the modern idea of what Santa Claus looks like.

Cartoon Comparisons   page 115

If this activity is to be done with ten or more students, collect suitable editorial cartoons over a period of two or three weeks before the assignment. Have students work in groups of two or three, using three or four different cartoons.

Most editorial cartoons involve an analogy of some kind. The analogy begins—or should begin—with real-life facts. The identification of those facts is extremely important. Since editorial cartoons often state strong, exaggerated opinions, it is critical that the reader understand the underlying factual situation. This activity could also be used in conjunction with a discussion of metaphor or simile.

Bonus! An analogy points out similarities.

Opinionated Pictures   page 116

This activity will work especially well following the study of a controversial news issue or event. The more familiarity students have with the topic, the stronger their opinions and perceptions will be. This activity provides an alternative to writing a letter to the editor—or it may be used to generate ideas for writing such a letter.

The synthesis of detail through a study of the characters involved in an event, possible symbols, and the activities that make up the event provides a systematic approach to critical thinking. The cartoon offers a way for students to visualize the interaction of variables in complex situations.

Bonus! The editorial cartoon appeared first, as caricatures, in ancient Egypt. In 1775, Benjamin Franklin drew a cartoon urging the colonies to unite against the French and Indians. By the mid-1800s, political cartoons were appearing regularly in some magazines. The first true comic strip, "The Little Bears and Tigers," appeared in 1892. Newspaper comic strips began appearing regularly in the *New York World* in 1894 and 1895, including "Origin of a New Species" and "Hogan's Alley."

Foto Facts   page 117

Students may have the idea that there are only two types of information, fact and opinion. This activity demonstrates that much of "fact," what we think we *know*, is really only inference.

To introduce the activity, have students identify facts about the photos as quickly as they can while you list them on the board or overhead projector. Do this *without* editing their ideas. Then help them understand the difference between fact and inference by doing step 2 together, going through their list of "facts" one by one. Do this first without the help of a news story or photo caption. Students should begin to see that the information we take in as "fact" may be mixed with considerable *inference*—our interpretation of what *may* be going on, based on our own ideas, beliefs, and values.

Bonus! A candid photo is probably closer to the truth than a posed one.

Just Picture That!   page 118

As students begin to work with step 1, they may write things like the following: "I know someone was hurt. I know there was an accident. I know the accident was caused by the weather." Before proceeding to step 2, challenge some of the statements students have written: "How do you *know* someone was hurt? Maybe they were taken to the hospital uninjured. How do you *know* it was an accident? Maybe it's a picture of a test car, or a paramedic training session. What makes you think it was caused by the weather? Maybe a car swerved to miss a dog in the road." Students may then want to revise their lists of things they "know" before continuing the activity. In doing step 2, students should be more cautious about jumping to conclusions. As an extension, discuss whether words are more factual than pictures.

Bonus! TV news is short on detail and is transitory—you can't sit and study it at your leisure as you can a newspaper—but it may lend more immediacy and authenticity to the news than print does.

Newsschool
LEARNING FROM LIFE

BOOK MAKING

1. Cut four sheets of 8½ by 11 inch paper in half to make eight sheets, 8½ by 5½ inches. Fold the eight sheets and staple them in the fold to make a little booklet.

2. Find and cut out 26 words or pictures from headlines and ads that match a single idea: a word for each of the 26 letters of the alphabet, 26 words that start like your name, 26 science words, 26 happy or sad words, 26 well-known names, etc.

3. Think of a good title for your book and make a cover design. Put your name on the first page as the author. Decide how your words and pictures will be arranged.

4. Paste the words and pictures in your book, using the fronts and backs of each page after the cover and author pages. Add anything you want to make your book meaningful: a sentence for each word, drawings, poetry, explanations or descriptions.

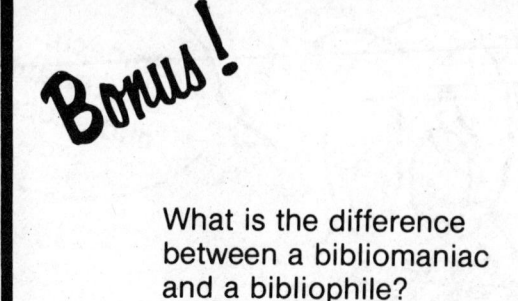

Bonus!

What is the difference between a bibliomaniac and a bibliophile?

About 10 pounds..

Copyright © 1984 by Dale Seymour Publications

Newsschool
LEARNING FROM LIFE

GROCERY LIST

Circle 30 different items in any one, large grocery ad. List the items in alphabetical order.

1. _____	16. _____
2. _____	17. _____
3. _____	18. _____
4. _____	19. _____
5. _____	20. _____
6. _____	21. _____
7. _____	22. _____
8. _____	23. _____
9. _____	24. _____
10. _____	25. _____
11. _____	26. _____
12. _____	27. _____
13. _____	28. _____
14. _____	29. _____
15. _____	30. _____

Bonus!

List 15 foods that begin with S.

Spinach, sauerkraut, and sausage!

Newsschool
LEARNING FROM LIFE

NAMES & NEWS WORDS

1. Find and print below 6 words in today's headlines and ads that begin with the same letter as your first name or last name.

   a. _____
   b. _____
   c. _____
   d. _____
   e. _____
   f. _____

2. List the letters of the alphabet that do not appear anywhere in the 6 words you found.

   ___ ___ ___ ___ ___
   ___ ___ ___ ___ ___

3. List words from today's front page that *do* contain the missing letters.

   a. _____
   b. _____
   c. _____
   d. _____

Bonus!

How many of the 26 letters of the alphabet are contained in your full name?

Quite a few if your name is Herkimer Hedgeworth Harquins.

Copyright © 1984 by Dale Seymour Publications

Newsschool
LEARNING FROM LIFE

ALPHABETICAL ORDERS
ABCD

Find in today's newspaper three words that begin with the letters listed. As you find them, write the three words in the "Word" Columns. Then number the words, according to alphabetical order, in the last column.

	Word	Word	Word	Order
A	America	automobile	Adams	2-3-1
B				
C				
D				
F				
L				
M				
P				
R				
S				
T				
W				

Bonus!

What does ALPHA mean?

It's a short form of alphalfa...?

Newsschool
LEARNING FROM LIFE

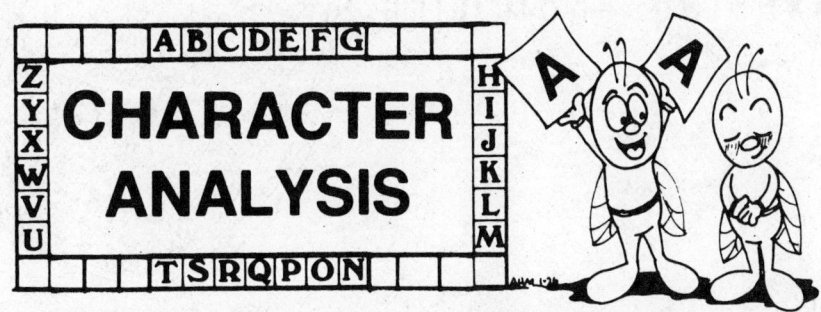

CHARACTER ANALYSIS

1. Find in today's paper adjectives (describing words) for each letter of the alphabet.

   a_____ j_____ s_____
   b_____ k_____ t_____
   c_____ l_____ u_____
   d_____ m_____ v_____
   e_____ n_____ w_____
   f_____ o_____ x_____
   g_____ p_____ y_____
   h_____ q_____ z_____
   i_____ r_____

2. List first and last names of people on today's front page and match their initials with the descriptors above!

   Name   Descriptors
   _____ = _____ and _____
   _____ = _____ and _____
   _____ = _____ and _____

Bonus!

What words that begin with your initials best describe you?

Nice and Beneficial!

Newsschool
LEARNING FROM LIFE

KEY WORDS

1. Circle all of the words in the main story on today's front page that would be found in a dictionary between AS and DO.
   If a word appears more than once, circle it only once.

   Count the words: _____

2. From the words you circled, list those that are key words in understanding the topic of the story.

Bonus!

What do you "see" first in a picture?
   a. nouns
   b. verbs
   c. adjectives

Interjections!

6 Copyright © 1984 by Dale Seymour Publications

Newsschool
LEARNING FROM LIFE

WORD WEBS

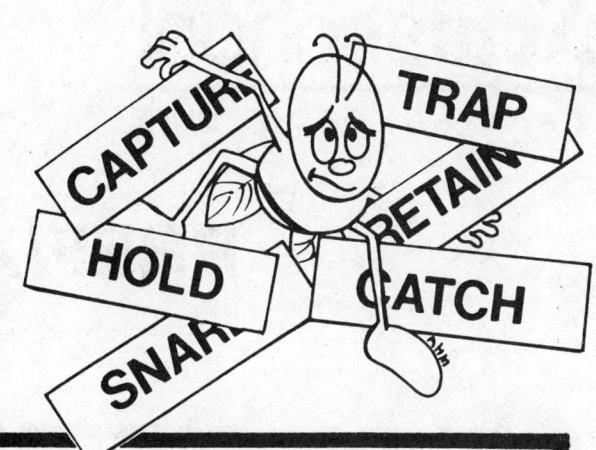

CAPTURE TRAP HOLD RETAIN CATCH SNARE

From anywhere in today's paper find words that are alike and write them in the web. They can be related by prefix, by suffix, by meaning, by subject, by structure, etc. Be sure to give your "word web" a title that identifies the relationship.

Title:

Bonus!

List the ways that these two words are alike:

dogs — cats

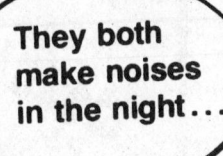

They both make noises in the night...

Copyright © 1984 by Dale Seymour Publications

Newsschool
LEARNING FROM LIFE

PREFIXING!

UN·
RE·
OVER·
PRE·
A·
·DO

---

1. From today's paper find and list at least 8 different words that have a *prefix*.

   Resigns   inmates   Exports

   a. _____
   b. _____
   c. _____
   d. _____
   e. _____
   f. _____
   g. _____
   h. _____

2. What is the most common *prefix* in your list? _____

   What does that prefix mean?

3. Select any words from your list of 8 and make 4 new words by changing prefixes:

   a. _____
   b. _____
   c. _____
   d. _____

Bonus!

Write two words that you think would be similar in meaning to "unfix."

What they unfix, I refix.

Newsschool
LEARNING FROM LIFE

SUFFIXED

1. From today's paper find and list at least 8 different words that have a *suffix*.

   Safely   Killed   Following

   a. _____
   b. _____
   c. _____
   d. _____
   e. _____
   f. _____
   g. _____
   h. _____

2. What is the most common suffix on your list? _____

   Why do you think that suffix is most popular?

3. Switch suffixes on any four words from your list and write the new words:

   a. _____
   b. _____
   c. _____
   d. _____

Bonus!

Fill in the appropriate suffixes to make a sentence:
The fix___ fix___ the fix___.

What a fix to be in!

Copyright © 1984 by Dale Seymour Publications

Newsschool
LEARNING FROM LIFE

SYL-LA-BLES

news- -pa- -per

1. Find and write 1 one-syllable word and 2 two-syllable words from today's newspaper.
   One _____
   Two _____
   _____

2. Find 3 three-syllable and 4 four-syllable words:
   Three _____
   _____
   _____
   Four _____
   _____
   _____
   _____

3. Find 5 five-syllable words:
   _____
   _____
   _____
   _____
   _____

4. List 6 six-syllable words, and if you find a word that contains *more* than six syllables, give yourself an additional 4 points!

Bonus!

How many syllables are there in SUPERCALIFRAGILISTICEXPIALIDOCIOUS and what does it mean?

That's what I call warm apple pie a la mode.

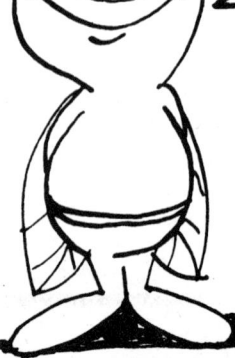

10 Copyright © 1984 by Dale Seymour Publications

Newsschool
LEARNING FROM LIFE

BIG (Voluminous) WORDS

negotiations
investigation
traditional
Commissioner
ratification

1. Print below 8 words in today's paper that contain *at least* 10 letters.
   a. _____
   b. _____
   c. _____
   d. _____
   e. _____
   f. _____
   g. _____
   h. _____

2. Put brackets [ ] around every prefix and suffix, and write what you think is the basic or root word:
   a. _____
   b. _____
   c. _____
   d. _____
   e. _____
   f. _____
   g. _____
   h. _____

3. Which word is least familiar to you? _____
   Write its dictionary definition: _____
   _____

Bonus!

Which of the five big words in the picture at the top of this page means *approval*?

Volumination is a bad habit...

GAB GAB GAB GAB

Copyright © 1984 by Dale Seymour Publications

Newsschool
LEARNING FROM LIFE

OPPO-WORDS

MOON LIGHT

1. Find and list nine compound words from today's paper.

2. Create "oppo-words" by writing the opposite of one part of each compound word.

3. Define each oppo-word and write a story that uses all of your new "oppo-words"!

	Compound Words	Oppo-words
a.	DOWNTOWN	UPTOWN
b.		
c.		
d.		
e.		
f.		
g.		
h.		
i.		

Bonus!

Is there a compound word in the instructions of this activity?

Maybe...

12 Copyright © 1984 by Dale Seymour Publications

Newsschool
LEARNING FROM LIFE

COMMON AND PROPER NAMES

1. List six words in stories on today's front page that are *capitalized* but *do not* begin a sentence.

   a. _____
   b. _____
   c. _____
   d. _____
   e. _____
   f. _____

2. Write a *less specific* name for each of the words you have listed.

   a. leader
   b. _____
   c. _____
   d. _____
   e. _____
   f. _____

Bonus!

Which of these words should be capitalized?
a. math
b. history
c. english
d. home ec

Copyright © 1984 by Dale Seymour Publications

Newsschool
LEARNING FROM LIFE

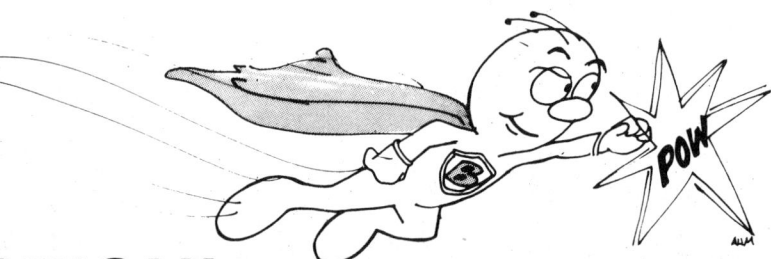

ACTION!

1. List eight lively action words in any sports story or feature story in today's paper. The words will probably be those that trigger word pictures in your mind.

2. For each verb, think of another stronger word to describe that same kind of action. Insert your livelier verbs into the original story. How do your words change the story?

LIVELY VERBS	LIVELIER VERBS
1.	
2.	
3.	
4.	
5.	
6.	
7.	
8.	

Bonus!

Which of these verbs is least like the others in meaning?
- trounced
- smashed
- threatened
- flattened

If I'm the direct object, I know which action I'd prefer...

Newsschool
LEARNING FROM LIFE

SYNONYMS & ANTONYMS

1. Select 3 words from headlines on today's front page and for each one find or write an antonym (a word that means the opposite).

   a. _____ b. _____ c. _____

   Ant. _____ **Ant.** _____ **Ant.** _____

2. Select 3 words from today's headlines and for each one find or write a synonym (a word that means the same or nearly the same).

   a. _____ b. _____ c. _____

   Syn. _____ **Syn.** _____ **Syn.** _____

3. From the sports pages, list all the words than mean "win" and all the words that mean "lose."

Bonus!

Are these two words synonyms or antonyms?

escape   capture

Look like verbs to me...

Copyright © 1984 by Dale Seymour Publications

Newsschool
LEARNING FROM LIFE

FOOLING AROUND

1. Find the "Homes for Sale" classified ads in today's paper. Read through several of the ads and circle the *words that describe* the house, certain rooms, the view, the neighborhood, etc.

2. List six of the descriptive words (adjectives) for which you know an *opposite* word (antonym), and then write the name of the thing being described (noun).

Adjective	Antonym	Noun
1.		
2.		
3.		
4.		
5.		
6.		

Bonus!

Would you take the house you've just re-described—even if someone *gave* it to you?

No Way!

Newsschool
LEARNING FROM LIFE

BOUT
MEDALIST
VICTORY
CHAMPION

SKIM & SCAN

In today's sports section search for these words and circle them when you find them. Give yourself one point for each one that you find.

homer	match	goalkeeper
putts	default	coach
pinned	average	pitcher
birdies	par	team
hitters	heavyweight	goalie
season	attitude	tournament
lost	won	players
score	training	game
shot	championship	strokes
fight	league	round
track	boxing	tennis
golf	baseball	basketball
wrestling	football	soccer
gymnastics	hockey	swimming

Bonus!

Who works at playing?
- professionals
- amateurs

The winners!

Copyright © 1984 by Dale Seymour Publications

17

Newsschool
LEARNING FROM LIFE

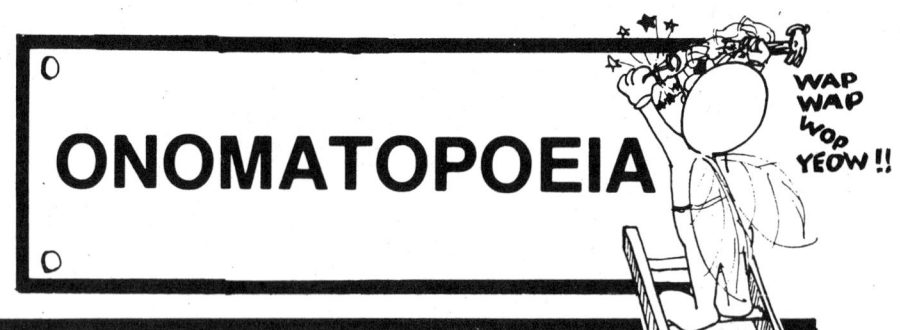

ONOMATOPOEIA

WAP WAP WOP YEOW!!

1. Clip "sound words" from today's headlines and ads. Separate the words into two categories:

   Quiet words   **Noisy words**

2. Arrange your "sound" words into a poem. Add your own words to those from the newspaper in order to finish your poem. Illustrate it.

Bonus!

How can you make ordinary words seem loud in print?

Ask for 120 point type!

18   Copyright © 1984 by Dale Seymour Publications

Newsschool
LEARNING FROM LIFE

ACRONYMS ETC.

1. An acronym like NATO is formed from the initial letters of parts of words. For example: N(orth) A(tlantic) T(reaty) O(rganization). Find and list four other familiar acronyms or initials used in today's paper and tell what they stand for.

   ACRONYMS OR INITIALS   MEANING

   1. _____   _____

   2. _____   _____

   3. _____   _____

   4. _____   _____

2. Explain how acronyms and initials *help* communications. How do they *hinder* communications?

Bonus!

Some say the word NEWS is actually an acronym. If so, what could the letters stand for?

Never Ever Write Sloppy?

Newsschool
LEARNING FROM LIFE

GENERALLY SPEAKING...

1. Find in today's paper *more specific* words for each word listed as shown in (a).

	General	Specific
a.	city	Seoul
b.	issue	
c.	citizen	
d.	job	
e.	ANIMAL	
f.	show	

2. Find more *general* terms for each of these words.

	General	Specific
a.		GREYHOUND
b.		Toyota
c.		Oregon

Bonus!

Which of these words is most specific? Most general?
a. male
b. human
c. President
d. leader

Must be talking about us . . .

20   Copyright © 1984 by Dale Seymour Publications

Newsschool
LEARNING FROM LIFE

SCRAMBLED STORIES

1. Select and cut out of today's paper a fairly long, interesting feature story. Paste the story to a piece of heavy paper or cardboard.

2. Measure and cut the story into 5 cm segments. Be careful to cut *inside* paragraphs, not *between* paragraphs.

> LOS ANGELES (AP) — Flooding closed the busy Santa Ana Freeway during the morning rush hour today after a Pacific storm dropped 2.74 inches of
>
> rain on Los Angeles in 24 hours. Some stranded motorists had to be helped from their cars on other freeways. Power was knocked out temporar-
>
> ily to about 7,000 customers, and two highway deaths were attributed to the storm.

3. Number each segment on the back in proper order. Mix up the pieces and see if you can beat the egg-timer in putting them back together!

Bonus!

Which part comes next, A or B?

> BOSTON — It was a vanquishing the likes of which will rewrite record books in both cities, but the individuals

A. humiliation of the Philadelphia 76ers Sunday was, as Sixers Coach Billy

B. involved preferred to classify the trouncing as an exception to the norm.

> In short, the Boston Celtics' 121-81

It was a vanquishing??

Copyright © 1984 by Dale Seymour Publications

Newsschool
LEARNING FROM LIFE

TYPES OF SENTENCES

1. In today's paper find, cut out, and label examples of the four basic sentence types:
   a. Declarative: one that makes a statement.
   b. Interrogative: one that asks a question.
   c. Imperative: one that gives a command.
   d. Exclamatory: one that exclaims.

2. Which of the four types of sentences appears most often in comic strips? Which type is most common on page one?

3. Can you find and circle all four types on the editorial page?

Bonus!

When a judge interrogates a witness, what does the witness get?

Nervous!

22 Copyright © 1984 by Dale Seymour Publications

Newsschool
LEARNING FROM LIFE

etc. WORD SEARCH

1. Copy five headlines from today's front page. Add words that are omitted but understood.

    a.

    b.

    c.

    d.

    e.

2. Put a check mark beside any of these structures you see in the headlines:

    ____ subject-verb-object pattern
    ____ noun made into a verb
    ____ verb made into a noun
    ____ noun used as an adjective
    ____ a question or command
    ____ a prepositional phrase
    ____ more than one pronoun
    ____ a clause

Bonus!

Bicycle sales in U.S. in excess of $1 billion

What words are omitted but understood?

It's called "reading between the words..."

Copyright © 1984 by Dale Seymour Publications

Newsschool
LEARNING FROM LIFE

DOUBLE MEANING

1. Circle and list words or phrases in today's headlines that don't *really* mean exactly what they say.

   Session planned for those hoping to sit on board

2. What do the words mean *literally*, as we commonly use each word?

3. What do the words mean *figuratively*, as we have come to know it in this context?

Word/Phrase	Literal Meaning	Figurative Meaning
1.		
2.		
3.		
4.		

Bonus!

What is an idiom?

Sometimes I feel like one...

Newsschool
LEARNING FROM LIFE

WORKS OF ART

1. To *design, build, decorate,* and *landscape* a home is an art. In today's classified ads for homes underline and list seven different words or phrases that describe these works of art.

   a. _____
   b. _____
   c. _____
   d. _____
   e. _____
   f. _____
   g. _____

2. Find articles or descriptions of *dramatic, musical,* or *artistic* events that are also considered "works of art." List words that describe them.

   a. _____
   b. _____
   c. _____
   d. _____
   e. _____
   f. _____
   g. _____
   h. _____

Bonus!

☐ True   ☐ False

All of these men were talented artists:
- Norman Rockwell
- Grant Wood
- Winston Churchill
- Rembrandt

Churchill created quite a scene in 1940, I know...

Copyright © 1984 by Dale Seymour Publications

Newsschool
LEARNING FROM LIFE

EXAGGERATION

1. Find and cut out of today's paper four examples of exaggeration: statements or pictures that *overstate* an idea or fact.

2. Tell what the artist or writer has exaggerated in each example.

3. Find the editorial cartoon and label the exaggerations in it.

LET US TAKE A LOAD OFF

4. Explain why you think writers and artists like to use exaggeration to communicate ideas. Is it fair? Does everyone use exaggeration at times to communicate?

Bonus!

List 3 other common phrases of exaggeration:
1. "A mile a minute..."
2.
3.
4.

Like—mm—I'm one in a million?

26 Copyright © 1984 by Dale Seymour Publications

Newsschool
LEARNING FROM LIFE

MAKING COMPARISONS

1. Circle words in headlines that don't really mean what they actually say.

   Select one headline and draw a picture of what the headline *actually*, literally says.

2. Select one sports headline and two other headlines from today's paper that contain an indirect comparison. Copy the headline below and state the comparison.

	HEADLINE	COMPARISON
a.		is like
b.		is like
c.		is like

Bonus!

The headline LIONS SCARE BEARS probably means:
- something happened at the zoo.
- one team almost beat another.
- researchers have made a new discovery.

"Lions scare bugs, too!!"

Copyright © 1984 by Dale Seymour Publications

Newsschool
LEARNING FROM LIFE

THE FAMOUS 4 W'S

WHO
WHAT WHEN
WHERE

1. The first sentence or paragraph of most news stories tells who, what, where, when. Underline the 4 W's in each news story on page one of today's paper.

Fire breaks out at Holiday Inn in Los Angeles

LOS ANGELES (AP) — A fire broke out today on the top floor of a hotel, forcing the evacuation of all 521 guests, officials said. One minor injury was reported.

The fire broke out about 7 a.m. on the top floor of the 12-story Holiday Inn about a mile from Los Angeles International Airport, and was declared controlled about a half-hour later. The fire, which issued dense black smoke, was confined to the room where it started, Fire Department spokesman Steve Ventura said.

No one was reported registered at the room where the fire started.

One private guard who suffered smoke inhalation was given oxygen by fire department paramedics at the scene and did not require hospitalization, Ventura said.

2. List the 4 W's from one of the stories.

Who _____
What _____
Where _____
When _____

3. Without looking back at the story, write one sentence that contains all 4 facts. Compare your version with the original.

Bonus!

What is the first paragraph of a news story called?

L _ _ D

News stories get called a lot of things...

Newsschool
LEARNING FROM LIFE

THE BIG IDEAS

1. State the *main idea* of the largest story in today's sports section.

2. State the *main ideas* of the two largest stories on today's front page.

3. State the *main idea* of the editorial cartoon on today's editorial page.

4. State the *main idea* of the first editorial on today's editorial page.

Bonus!

The main idea of Humpty Dumpty is:
a. High walls are dangerous.
b. Accidents can be fatal.
c. Some things can't be fixed no matter how hard we try.

Humpty got dumped, that's all...

Copyright © 1984 by Dale Seymour Publications

Newsschool
LEARNING FROM LIFE

SIMPLY SAY IT!

1. Find and cut out of today's paper 3 short (2-3 inches long), one-column news stories. Cut off their headlines *immediately*.

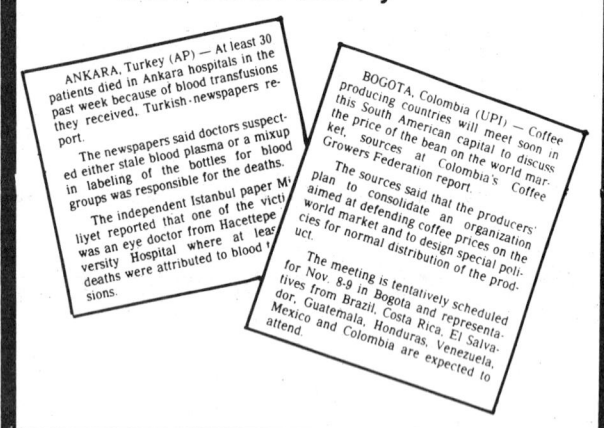

2. With the headlines gone, read each article and write headlines for them. Be sure your headline (a) states the main idea of the article and (b) has a subject and a verb.

3. Compare your headlines to the original three. They probably won't be the same, but they should be similar!

Bonus!

On April 15, 1912, this headline appeared in newspapers. What was the subject?

"_____ Sinks"

And no one's seen it since . . .

30 Copyright © 1984 by Dale Seymour Publications

Newsschool
LEARNING FROM LIFE

ONCE UPON A TIME...

1. Find an article in today's paper that gives a time or day in which something happened or was accomplished: minute by minute, hour by hour, day by day, or year by year.

2. Fill in the first and last things and the five most important events in between.

   First • _____
   _____
   • _____
   • _____
   • _____
   • _____
   • _____
   Last • _____
   _____

3. Do most news stories begin by telling the first thing that happened or the most important thing that happened?

Bonus!

The first sentence or paragraph of a news story usually contains the 4 W's. What are the 4 W's?

Wow! Willikers! Whee! Whew!

Copyright © 1984 by Dale Seymour Publications

Newsschool
LEARNING FROM LIFE

COMPREHENSION CLUES

1. Find an article in today's paper about an accident or crime.

   List a sequence of 10 actions (how things happened) from start to finish, as you *think* they occurred.

2. Check the items on your list that you *know* for a *fact*.

   The unchecked items are "inferences." Do detectives need to know how to *infer*?

TIME	ACT	TIME	ACT
__:__	_____	__:__	_____
__:__	_____	__:__	_____
__:__	_____	__:__	_____
__:__	_____	__:__	_____
__:__	_____	__:__	_____

Bonus!

Are most "rumors" facts or inferences?

...or a little of both...

32 Copyright © 1984 by Dale Seymour Publications

Newsschool
LEARNING FROM LIFE

WRITING FOR A REASON

1. Number and list the *titles* of four editorials, columns, or letters on today's editorial page. Underline the words in each piece of writing that identify the *topic*.

2. Which term best describes the writer's *purpose* in each of the four writings?
   - to inform
   - to entertain
   - to criticize
   - to praise
   - to persuade
   - to illustrate

3. How well do you think each writer achieved the intended purpose? Rate the success of each writing.

   1 poor
   2 problems
   3 good
   4 excellent

Title	Purpose	Success
1.		1 2 3 4
2.		1 2 3 4
3.		1 2 3 4
4.		1 2 3 4

Bonus!

How would you describe the best book you've ever read?
a. informative
b. dramatic
c. humorous

"Short!"

Copyright © 1984 by Dale Seymour Publications

33

Newsschool
LEARNING FROM LIFE

FACTS AND OPINIONS

1. Cut out of today's paper one editorial and one letter to the editor that contain:

   FACTS (statements that can be proven true or false).

   OPINIONS (statements of belief or feeling that cannot yet be proven true or false).

2. Circle the opinions. Underline the facts.

3. Check the statements that are *true*.
   - [ ] Facts are easier to recognize than opinions.
   - [ ] Facts and opinions can be combined into a single statement that seems factual.
   - [ ] Letters to the editor are more *fact* than *opinion*.
   - [ ] Editorials are more *opinion* than fact.

Bonus!

Everybody knows that men are braver than women. Is that a fact?

Who dares prove it?!

SQUEAK

# Newsschool
LEARNING FROM LIFE

ONE PERSON'S OPINION

Cut out of today's paper any interesting item on the editorial page that expresses a strong opinion. State the topic, the opinion, facts presented to support the opinion, and questions still unanswered in your mind.

Topic	Opinion	Facts	Questions

Bonus!

What is an "informed opinion"?

Someone else told them what to think...

Newsschool
LEARNING FROM LIFE

VIEWPOINTS

1. Cut out all of the stories you can find in today's paper that are *all* related to the same event or issue.

2. Why would a newspaper print more than one article about the same event? How is each article different?

3. How many of these writing styles or purposes are represented by the articles you clipped?
   - News
   - Feature
   - Letter
   - Interview
   - Editorial
   - Review
   - Analysis

4. Choose one of the stories on today's page one, and describe three or four other viewpoints of the event or issue that could be developed into additional articles.

Bonus!

How much can be written about a strawberry?

In which language...?

Newsschool
LEARNING FROM LIFE

TWO SIDES TO EVERY STORY

1. Find an incident described in today's paper. It might be in a news story, in letters to the editor, or in letters asking advice.

2. Whose viewpoint is presented? Who might have a different point of view on the same topic?

3. Write a letter or response to the incident presenting a different point of view. In your response, don't deny any of the incident; just present your own explanations of how and why.

Bonus!

Why is it important to look at both sides of a story?

If you don't, you might miss the best part!

FACTS FIND DEFENDANT INNOCENT

Copyright © 1984 by Dale Seymour Publications

Newsschool
LEARNING FROM LIFE

READ & REACT

1. Read through today's paper and, using a colored marker, indicate *which* and *how much* of the headlines, stories, and ads you read.

2. Return to three or four stories or ads that really caught and held your attention. What made those items appeal more?

3. Because those articles created strong feelings in you, you may have something to say about one of those topics. Say it in a letter to the editor.

4. Can you imagine that some reader might feel just the opposite about the topic? Write a letter to the editor from that person's point of view.

Bonus!

"Bias" in reading and writing refers to:
a. prejudice.
b. preference.
c. slant.
d. all of the above.

That's poor advertising!!

Newsschool
LEARNING FROM LIFE

I'M AGAINST IT! RIGHT ON!

1. Find two articles or letters to the editor that contain statements *against* something. Tell what is being opposed in each situation and give the reasons.

2. What are some points about the topic that are not mentioned? Do you agree or disagree with the opposition? Give your viewpoints on each topic. Try to see both sides.

ITEM A

OPPOSED TO: _____

_____

_____

BECAUSE: _____

_____

_____

ITEM B

OPPOSED TO: _____

_____

_____

BECAUSE: _____

_____

_____

Bonus!

What is your definition of "healthy" criticism?

All criticism that isn't aimed at me!

Copyright © 1984 by Dale Seymour Publications

Newsschool
LEARNING FROM LIFE

DEAR EDITOR...

1. Find and cut out all of the letters to the editor in today's paper.

2. For each letter state in one sentence the writer's purpose for the letter.

3. How many of the letters do the following?
   - criticize _____
   - praise _____
   - inform _____
   - entertain _____
   - persuade _____
   - other _____

4. Write a response to one of the letters offering a viewpoint different from the writer's.

Bonus!

Who is the editor of the newspaper you are reading?

Someone in a green visor.

Newsschool
LEARNING FROM LIFE

☐ AGREE
☐ DISAGREE
☐ wishy-washy

1. List the topics people have written about in today's letters to the editor.

2. Cut out a letter with which you mostly agree and one with which you mostly disagree.

3. In the "agree letter," underline the *best* sentence in the letter. What do you like about the sentence?

4. In the "disagree letter," underline the sentence with which you disagree the most. Write a response to the letter and *send* it.

Bonus!

What does the word "forum" mean?

A place for me to prove I'm right!

Copyright © 1984 by Dale Seymour Publications

Newsschool
LEARNING FROM LIFE

"BEAUTY"

1. Select and cut out of today's paper *your own opinion* of

   (a) a beautiful *word*.
   (b) a beautiful *picture*.
   (c) a beautiful *person*.
   (d) a beautiful *idea*.

   Explain what is beautiful to you about each of your selections.

2. Find and cut out a picture or an ad of a *machine* that others might consider beautiful, but that you don't care for. Tell why.

3. What does this statement mean to you? "Beauty is in the eye of the beholder."

Bonus!

What did John Keats say about beauty in "Ode on a Grecian Urn"?

Everything he knew... and all we need to know...

42 Copyright © 1984 by Dale Seymour Publications

Newsschool
LEARNING FROM LIFE

SETTING

1. Find two stories in today's paper that feature a dramatic event. Would either story have been any different if it had happened 10 years ago? 20 years ago?

2. Where did each story happen? Could it have happened any place else? Does city or geography make a difference to the story?

3. What time of day did it happen? Would a different time of day have made a difference?

4. Who are the people involved in each story? What if they had been younger or older, richer or poorer, more educated or less educated?

Bonus!

What if you had been born 10 years later than you were?

I'd be young again!

Copyright © 1984 by Dale Seymour Publications

Newsschool
LEARNING FROM LIFE

STATIC & DYNAMIC CHARACTERS

1. List three comic strip characters in today's paper with whom you are most familiar. Now read the definitions for static and dynamic characters.

2. Decide which type each character is and cite reasons for your answer. How is character type important to the strip?

TYPES OF CHARACTERS

STATIC — Those who change very little on the inside, regardless of what's happening on the outside.

DYNAMIC — Those whose values and personalities change because of certain events and people entering their lives.

CHARACTER	TYPE	EVIDENCE

Bonus!

What are FLAT or ROUND characters in novels?

Sounds like another diet book...

44 Copyright © 1984 by Dale Seymour Publications

Newsschool
LEARNING FROM LIFE

THE BEGINNING AND ENDING

1. Cut out any news story on page one of today's paper. Put the name of the happening in the center of the wheel.

2. In each section of the wheel describe something that may have led up to the story in today's paper.

3. Where and when do you think this event will eventually end?

4. Which more accurately describes the news: NEWS EVENTS or NEWS DEVELOPMENTS? Explain your choice.

Bonus!

What's wrong with reading the news "once in awhile"?

You might suffer a lapse...

YESTERDAY TODAY

Copyright © 1984 by Dale Seymour Publications

45

Newsschool
LEARNING FROM LIFE

PRESUMING & PREDICTING

1. Find an article in today's paper that "predicts" tomorrow's weather. Do "forecast" and "predict" mean the same thing?

2. What "clues" does the weatherman have *today* about tomorrow's weather?

3. Find a news article anywhere in today's paper that provides clues about a future event. Underline the clues.

4. Write your prediction. When will a follow-up story on that event probably appear? Check that day's paper to find out the accuracy of your prediction.

Bonus!

What is "intuition"?

A cognitive surprise!

Newsschool
LEARNING FROM LIFE

SUSPENSE!

1. Find a suspenseful article in today's paper — an article that has unresolved conflict.

2. Describe the parts of the story that intrigue you and make you want more information.

3. State the question uppermost in your mind that you want answered. List three ways you might satisfy your desire to know.

   a.

   b.

   c.

Bonus!

Who did Sir Arthur Conan Doyle introduce to the public as the most famous detective in fiction?

That's a mystery in itself!

The Case of the Missing Miss

Copyright © 1984 by Dale Seymour Publications

Newsschool
LEARNING FROM LIFE

TO BE CONTINUED...

1. Cut out and read carefully the most *interesting local* news story in today's paper. Why does the story interest you?

2. List two or three questions about the event that you hope future stories will answer.

   a.

   b.

   c.

3. Does the story in today's paper really describe "the beginning" or "the end" of the event, or is it only a piece of a longer story?

Bonus!

Is it possible to tell "all" about an event?

In 25 words or less??

Newsschool
LEARNING FROM LIFE

SENTENCING!

Bank raises rate

1. Cut out 4 headlines on page one of today's paper. Cut each headline between the subject part and the part that comments about the subject. Scramble the headline parts.

2. See if someone else can match up the headline pieces. See if *you* can make up two *new* headlines from the headline pieces.

Wild market
making changes effective Sunday
Transit district
doesn't panic area investors

3. Rewrite two of the headlines using only a one word subject and a one-word comment.

Bonus!

Can you write 20 complete sentences that contain no more than 2 words each?

That's simple! I'm smart!

Copyright © 1984 by Dale Seymour Publications

49

Newsschool
LEARNING FROM LIFE

PLAYING WITH WORDS

1. Find an article in today's paper that describes an event or situation you can picture in your mind. List names and actions that match the picture in your mind.

2. Write about the picture in your mind using two-word sentences composed of a one-word subject and a one-word verb.

3. Recreate the feelings or moods of the event or situation you have pictured in your mind by writing any two-word combinations.

4. Write in final form your version of the story as you have pictured it and described it in steps two and three.

Bonus!

Name this familiar story.
Children thirst.
Boy climbs.
Girl climbs. So sad.
Boy falls. Too bad.
Boy rolls. She's mad.
Boy breaks.
Girl imitates.

It can't be Adam and Eve...

50   Copyright © 1984 by Dale Seymour Publications

Newsschool
LEARNING FROM LIFE

SENSITIVITY

1. Find a picture in today's paper that *appeals* to you. List the things you see in the picture.

2. After each word on your list, write another word that further describes the first word.

3. Keep adding to the list of what you see and the words that describe what you see until you have said all that the picture shows.

4. Circle the 10 word combinations from your list that best say what the picture shows. Arrange those word combinations in a final form.

Bonus!

Which is more important to "seeing"?
- awareness
- concentration

Microscopic eyes would be helpful, too...

Copyright © 1984 by Dale Seymour Publications

Newsschool
LEARNING FROM LIFE

The *elderly* *man was a hero.*
The man was

SENTENCE COMBINING

1. Select and cut out the first paragraph of any two interesting stories in today's paper.

   Break down the first sentence of the story into many simple sentences, using one fact in each sentence. One simple sentence might tell who, another what, another when, another where, another why. For example: The rodeo is coming. It will be in the town. It will come on Friday.

2. Consider how many ways the reporter might have combined the facts of the simple sentences into one sentence. Write at least eight different possibilities.

3. Compare your eight sentences with the one the reporter actually used. Do you like any of yours better than the one printed in today's paper?

Bonus!

Combine these sentences into one sentence of 5 words.
   a. A girl had an animal.
   b. The girl's name was Mary.
   c. The animal was a lamb.
   d. The lamb was little.

"Mary, a girl, had a little animal which was a lamb."

"Had a lamb, little Mary?"

52 Copyright © 1984 by Dale Seymour Publications

Newsschool
LEARNING FROM LIFE

A FUNNY THING HAPPENED...

1. Select a humorous comic strip from today's paper in which two or more characters have a conversation.

2. Rewrite the comic strip as though it were a story. Be sure to introduce the characters, the setting, and the situation adequately, realizing that your reader will not see what you are seeing.

3. Double-check your writing for form and content:
   a. Did you place quotation marks around the words spoken by each person?
   b. Did you make a new paragraph each time the speaker changed?
   c. Did you add descriptive detail about tone of voice, volume, mannerisms, expressions, behavior?

Bonus!

Which would take more space in the paper: a cartoon or a written explanation of a cartoon?

Talk about drawing it out...

Copyright © 1984 by Dale Seymour Publications

Newsschool
LEARNING FROM LIFE

PARAGRAPHS—
EASY AS A·B·C

A.
ANNOUNCEMENT: State in one complete sentence what you think is the most interesting story in today's paper.

B.
BECAUSE: Add two or three sentences that tell why you find that story the most interesting.

C.
CONCLUSION: Finish by writing one more sentence that sums up, wraps up, or points up the announcement in the first sentence.

Bonus!

Can you write a sentence or paragraph with every word in alphabetical order?

Impossible!?

54   Copyright © 1984 by Dale Seymour Publications

Newsschool
LEARNING FROM LIFE

NO TWO ALIKE!

1. Cut out five different *drawings* (not photos) of people in today's paper and paste them on a sheet of paper.

    How are all five alike?

    How are all five different?

2. Cut out five *different* letters in headlines and ads of your first or last initial. Paste them on a sheet of paper. How are they all different?

3. Finish this paragraph.
   There are at least three reasons why differences in people and things are more exciting than similarities.

Bonus!

Which letter do you like best and why?

M M *m*

What a difference variety makes...

Copyright © 1984 by Dale Seymour Publications

55

Newsschool
LEARNING FROM LIFE

MAKING SENSE

1. Select any three articles from today's paper that interest you and label them A, B, C.

   Read all three stories carefully to pick up the main ideas.

2. Read the articles a second time to see how information is organized. Which of the methods listed below do you think the writer was using in each of the three stories?

Ways to Organize Information	A	B	C
(1) Most important to least important			
(2) Time sequence			
(3) Cause and effect			
(4) Comparison/contrast			
(5) _____			
(6) _____			

Bonus!

Which of these might be described by spatial sequence (what you see first or left to right)?
- a ball game
- a speech
- a fair

It depends on whether the speaker is far left or far right...

Newsschool
LEARNING FROM LIFE

READ ON! READ ON!

1. Cut out two stories in today's paper that have a "by-line" (a line under the headline that tells who wrote the article).

2. Copy the *first* paragraph of each story. What did the writer say (or not say) that makes you want to read on?

3. Copy the *last* paragraph of each story. Explain how the writer has successfully given the article a "final touch."

4. For writing to be good writing, what do you think it should do to or for the reader?

Bonus!

Which book begins: "It was the best of times, it was the worst of times…"?
- David Copperfield
- A Christmas Carol
- Tale of Two Cities

Dickens wrote about the 1980's?!

Copyright © 1984 by Dale Seymour Publications

Newsschool
LEARNING FROM LIFE

CREATE-A-CHARACTER

1. Cut out of today's paper six photographs of people. From your collection of pictures, select two and give them a first and last name of your own choosing.

2. Create a way for the two people to know each other. Describe their relationship.

3. Describe the best qualities of each character. Describe the weakest qualities of each character.

4. Write a quotation for each character: something each one might have just said that will reveal what that person is really like.

Bonus!

Agatha Christie got ideas for her characters from
- movies.
- newspapers.
- neighbors.

...how about nightmares!?!

Newsschool
LEARNING FROM LIFE

FACT & FICTION

1. Cut out a picture from today's paper and make up your own names, places, and details to answer:

   Who _____,
   What _____,
   Why _____,
   Where _____,
   When _____,
   How _____.

2. Think about the "facts" you have just written. If there is no suspense, or danger, or conflict involved, add some.

3. Now, using the "facts" above and the "plot," write your story about the picture.

Bonus!

Which part in a short story makes it most interesting?
- characters
- conflict
- climax

☐ characters
☐ conflict
☐ climax
☒ all of the

"Maybe it takes all 3!"

Copyright © 1984 by Dale Seymour Publications

Newsschool
LEARNING FROM LIFE

FACT & FANTASY

1. From the entertainment section of today's paper select the movie that most appeals to you and tell why you chose it.

   Title: _____
   I would like to see it because:
   _____
   _____
   _____
   _____

2. Select a movie you would **not** like to see and explain your choice.

   Title: _____
   I would not like to see it because _____
   _____
   _____
   _____

3. Which film seems more factual? Which film seems to contain more fantasy? Are both *fact* and *fantasy* useful in a good story?   Explain.

Bonus!

Finish Lord Byron's statement: "_____ is stranger than fiction."

Modern art??

Newsschool
LEARNING FROM LIFE

RHYME & REASON

1. Find two or three articles or pictures in today's paper that create strong feelings in you of love, fear, anger, etc.

2. For each of the stories you selected, write briefly and rapidly the *feelings* you get at seeing or reading or thinking about the item.

3. Take what you have written for one of the articles and polish the words and phrases into your *exact* feeling about the topic.

4. Arrange the words and phrases on paper in an orderly and interesting way for someone else to read and enjoy.

Bonus!

What is poetry in picture form called?
- free verse
- concrete poetry
- found poetry

Picturesque?

hills hills hills hills hills hills hills hills hills hills hills hills hills hills hills hills and more hills

Copyright © 1984 by Dale Seymour Publications

Newsschool
LEARNING FROM LIFE

THE HEART OF THE MATTER

1. Find a story in today's paper that involves feelings of love, joy, hate, anger, frustration, excitement, sadness, fear, or determination. List the strongest emotions in the story and tell which of the characters probably experienced those feelings and when.

Feelings	Character	Occasion

2. Write a scene that describes very specifically what the characters said and did at a moment of great emotion in the story. The emotional impact should be *felt* by the reader.

Bonus!

This activity should produce in the reader
- sympathy.
- empathy.
- telepathy.

How about apathy...

Newsschool
LEARNING FROM LIFE

GOOD SENSES

1. Find and number three articles in today's paper that describe an *unusual* experience someone has had. For each article tell what the main character heard, saw, tasted, smelled, or felt.

2. Select one of the articles and write a paragraph that describes *in detail* something seen, felt, heard, tasted, or smelled by one character.

	Sights	Sounds	Tastes	Smells	Feel/Touch
1.					
2.					
3.					

Bonus!

What do the initials E.S.P. stand for and what does it mean?

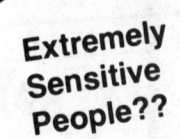

Extremely Sensitive People??

Copyright © 1984 by Dale Seymour Publications

Newsschool
LEARNING FROM LIFE

THE FIVE SENSES

1. Find and cut out pictures or ads in today's paper that represent each of the five senses: taste, feel, sight, smell, sound. Identify which of the senses each one represents.

2. Circle any words with the picture or ad that add sensory details.

   Compact low-cost alarm with protective lens, (easy-to-read) dial. Sweep second hand. Plain dial with a white finish.

3. Pretend that you must explain each picture to a person who has lost the sense that it represents. For example, how would you explain the picture representing 'sight' to a blind person?

   Pickled — The ancient alchemy of vinegary brine transforms garden-variety foods to delicacies

Bonus!

What is the 'sixth' sense?

I just know, you know..?

64 Copyright © 1984 by Dale Seymour Publications

Newsschool
LEARNING FROM LIFE

FACES WITH FEELINGS

1. Cut out of today's paper five pictures or illustrations of faces that show feelings.

2. Name the feeling each face shows and tell what you think is *causing* the feelings.

3. Write a short story involving any *two* of the faces. You can use conversation, action, and description to help the reader understand what is happening in your story.

Bonus! Which is really more expressive in a picture— eyes or mouth?

Don't know about a picture, but in real life...

Copyright © 1984 by Dale Seymour Publications

Newsschool
LEARNING FROM LIFE

FROM START TO FINISH

1. Cut out every sports picture in today's paper to study facial expressions. List the emotions that you see.

2. Select one picture and list the things the person heard, felt, saw, tasted, and smelled around the time the picture was taken.

3. Write the *thoughts* the person had from the start of an event to the end of an event. Use no more than one side of one sheet of paper. You may want to include ideas from the list of senses in step 2.

Bonus!

Writing a character's thoughts is called "stream of _____."

That describes my thoughts precisely: "_____".

66 Copyright © 1984 by Dale Seymour Publications

Newsschool
LEARNING FROM LIFE

LOST & FOUND

1. Read some of the ads in today's classified section under LOST AND FOUND. Try to imagine the reasons why certain ads appear.

2. Let your imagination run wild and list as many reasons as you can for any *two* of the ads. Clip the two ads and attach them to the lists.

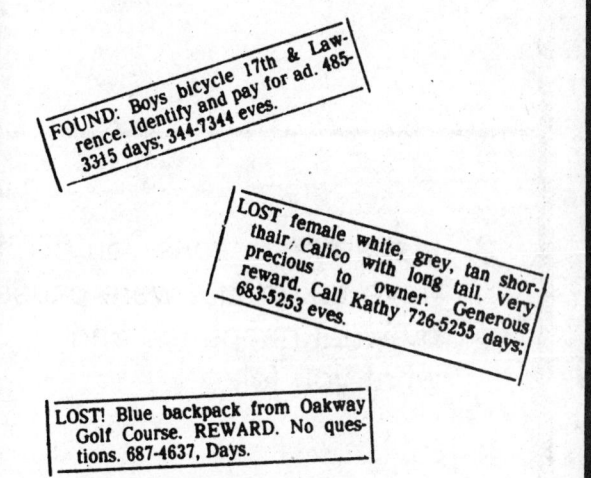

FOUND: Boys bicycle 17th & Lawrence. Identify and pay for ad. 485-3315 days; 344-7344 eves.

LOST female white, grey, tan shorthair, Calico with long tail. Very precious to owner. Generous reward. Call Kathy 726-5255 days; 683-5253 eves.

LOST! Blue backpack from Oakway Golf Course. REWARD. No questions. 687-4637, Days.

3. Create a first person story, telling how one of the things happened to be lost or found. Include vivid descriptions and strong feelings.

Bonus!

Lost and Found are:
a. homonyms.
b. synonyms.
c. antonyms.
d. zaponyms.

Zaponyms??

Newsschool
LEARNING FROM LIFE

YOU ARE THERE

1. Select a dramatic story from today's paper. *Imagine* yourself at the scene. List some things you would have seen, heard, smelled, felt, tasted.

2. List the *emotions* that would come to you in seeing, hearing, smelling, feeling, and tasting what you have listed.

3. List some *actions* you might have taken that were caused by what happened and what you felt.

4. Write a descriptive account of the event as though you were there. Build into your writing things from all three lists.

Bonus!

A piece of writing that tells a story is called:
- exposition.
- narrative.
- literary.
- poetic.

When I tell stories they're called fibs...

Newsschool
LEARNING FROM LIFE

YOU'RE KIDDING

1. Find a headline, ad, news story, or editorial that is only *half* serious.

   Underline the words that make you think the writer is playing with words—and with the reader.

   THE STORY OF CHICKEN BIG.

   Once upon a time there was a little chicken restaurant named Church's in San Antonio, Texas. Being from Texas where everybody thinks big, they never stopped to think little, but just started cooking the best fried chicken they could.

   The competition didn't notice. But customers did, because Church's had a special way of cooking their chicken.

2. Compare the half-serious item to a *very* serious news story. What are the clues that reveal the *tone* in a piece of writing?

3. Find a matter-of-fact article and rewrite it, using vocabulary and imagery that will give the story a light touch.

Bonus!

Define *satire*.

It's the birthstone for September, right?

Copyright © 1984 by Dale Seymour Publications

Newsschool
LEARNING FROM LIFE

WHADJA SAY??

1. Find and cut out of today's cartoons or ads examples of casual, informal, or non-standard language.

   > NO! NO! NO! NO BUN! **NO NOTHIN'!!!** HOW MANY TIMES I GOTTA TELL YA — I JUST WANT A PLAIN OLD NAKED HAMBURGER!!!

2. Find two ads in today's paper in which the language seems especially formal.

   > *These luxury looks can be yours for less than you imagine possible. Choose from a flattering palette, all of deep-pile fabric imitating mink.*

3. Rewrite an ad in informal, non-standard, slang form.

4. What attitude or tone does formal language convey? What does informal language convey?

Bonus! Rewrite the title of this activity in formal, standard English.

Eh??

Newsschool
LEARNING FROM LIFE

MIXED UP

1. Cut out of today's paper six different stories of high interest. Read quickly all six stories.

2. Just for fun, pretend that all of the paragraphs and sentences of the stories fell apart and had to be pieced together again. Construct a "new" story by mixing and rearranging parts from all six stories into one story.

"New" Story

Bonus!

If a piece of writing has coherence, it
- has deep meaning.
- has order and logic.
- sticks to the topic.

It means it's not incoherent...

Newsschool
LEARNING FROM LIFE

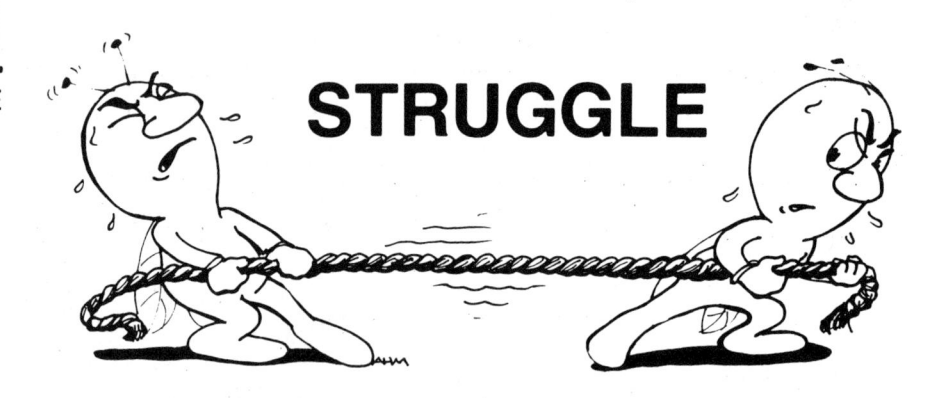

STRUGGLE

1. Find one example in today's paper for each of these types of struggle or conflict:

   a. Man against man.

   b. Man against nature.

   c. Man against society.

   d. Man against self.

2. Is conflict, as seen in each of your examples, good or bad? Explain your position.

3. Select one conflict and explain how the conflict could turn out to be a very valuable turning point in one person's life.

Bonus!

What would you say is the greatest conflict you've ever had?

Survival!

72 Copyright © 1984 by Dale Seymour Publications

Newsschool
LEARNING FROM LIFE

STRUGGLE AND STRIFE

1. Find and cut out four articles in today's paper that tell about a struggle or strife. What or who is involved in each situation?

2. What are the most valuable lessons or qualities that might be learned or strengthened through this situation?

Struggle or Strife	Values to be Learned
1.	
2.	
3.	
4.	

Bonus!

Describe the last 24 hours of your life but *omit* any conflict or difficulty.

How boring!

Copyright © 1984 by Dale Seymour Publications

Newsschool
LEARNING FROM LIFE

MISHAPS AND OTHER MISFORTUNES

Find and cut out four articles from today's news that tell about someone's misfortune. Read each article, describe the misfortune, and tell one thing that a person could learn from the misfortune described in the story.

a. Event: _____ Lesson: _____
   _____

b. Event: _____ Lesson: _____
   _____

c. Event: _____ Lesson: _____
   _____

d. Event: _____ Lesson: _____
   _____

Bonus!

Unscramble this quotation from Publilius Syrus.

He   another's   wise
truly   from   who
wisdom   is   mishap.
gains

And I can't call him and ask him, either.

74   Copyright © 1984 by Dale Seymour Publications

Newsschool
LEARNING FROM LIFE

CHOOSING OUR RESPONSES

1. Find two examples of the kinds of news that made someone's day bad. Find two examples of the kinds of news that made someone's day *good*.

2. How did the people in each story respond? Read the *"bad news"* articles and list the kinds of ways people responded to what happened.

3. Read the "good news" articles and list the kinds of ways people responded to what happened.

4. How would you have responded in each of the four situations? Would your response have been the same as theirs? Explain.

Bonus!

Who wrote, "If you can meet with Triumph and Disaster, and treat those two imposters just the same... You'll be a Man, my son!"

...a parent...

Copyright © 1984 by Dale Seymour Publications

Newsschool
LEARNING FROM LIFE

GOOD ONES & BAD ONES

1. Find a story in today's paper about someone who has done something good. Give the person's name and describe the good that was done.

2. Try to put yourself in that person's place and explain why you think the person did the good that was done. Was it difficult or easy?

3. Find a story in the paper about someone who has done something that most would label bad. Who is the person and what was done?

4. Put yourself in that person's place and explain what you think caused the person to do what was done. Was it difficult or easy?

Bonus!

Was "self-image" involved in the two stories you chose?

If you think your hat is black, it is??

Newsschool
LEARNING FROM LIFE

CHANGE OF A LIFETIME

1. Find in today's paper four events that changed the lives of the people involved. List the events and some of the changes that followed.

2. Describe some of the emotions and responses that might follow such a life-changing event.

3. Select one event and write a short story about how one person handled the changes.

Event	Change	Emotions/Responses
a.		
b.		
c.		
d.		

Bonus!

If you could make only one change in your life, what would it be and why?

The ability to accept what can't be changed...

Copyright © 1984 by Dale Seymour Publications

Newsschool
LEARNING FROM LIFE

UPS AND DOWNS

1. Find a feature article in today's paper that tells about a person's life—past and present. Indicate the person's *present* age on the line below. Read the article carefully and circle any dates of events in the person's life.

2. Indicate where these events would go on the life line below. If they are good, put them above the line; if bad, put them below the line.

3. Which event had the greatest impact on that person's life? Was it a turning point for the best —or the worst?

Birth 0 ——— 25 ——— 50 ——— 75 ——— 100

Bonus!

Make your own life line showing your ups and downs.

"No wonder I feel like a yo-yo!!"

Newsschool
LEARNING FROM LIFE

TURNING POINTS

1. Find in today's paper four different kinds of events that can happen in a person's life to *change* that life in some way.

2. For each event, indicate the age of the person involved and the name of the event on the time line below.

0   10   20   30   40   50   60   70   80   90

3. Select any *one* of the ages and events and tell how that event could be a turning point in that person's life.

Bonus!

What was the single most important turning point in your life this year?

Also known as mind-bending experiences??

Copyright © 1984 by Dale Seymour Publications

Newsschool
LEARNING FROM LIFE

MEANNESS VS. COURAGE

1. Find an article in today's paper in which someone has done something with "magnificent courage." What did the person do?

2. Find an article in which someone has done something with "incredible meanness." What did the person do?

3. Write your answer to any *one* of these three questions:

   a. Could/would you have done what the courageous one did?
   b. What were the motives of either person?
   c. What were the consequences of the courage and the meanness?

Bonus!

Explain what this famous quotation means: "Speak softly and carry a big stick."

Be courageous until you have to be mean...

Newsschool
LEARNING FROM LIFE

HE-ROES & HER-OES

1. Find and cut out two articles in today's paper about people who have great ability, strength, or courage.

2. Tell why you chose each article. What impresses you about the people involved?

3. Think of a time when you or someone you know did something somewhat similar to what happened in either of the articles.

   What happened? Who was there? What time of day was it? Where?

4. Write about the experience you have just remembered. Write it like a news story, telling who, what, where, when in the first paragraph. Then give more detail about each fact.

Bonus!

Which is *not* usually an element of heroism?
- wisdom
- luck
- strength
- position

Lucky thing I had a rope so I could be a hero...

Copyright © 1984 by Dale Seymour Publications

Newsschool
LEARNING FROM LIFE

HEROIC ACTION

1. Find an article in today's paper about an accident, fire, storm, or crime that put someone's life in danger.

2. Identify the person in the story who was most courageous, wise, loving, or strong in the actions taken.

3. List some of the things that person might have seen, heard, felt, tasted, or smelled during the most critical time of the event.

4. Write what that person might have written in a diary or journal after the event was all over.

Bonus!

What is an "unsung hero"?

Unsung or unstrung??!

Newsschool
LEARNING FROM LIFE

HELP FOR THE HAPLESS

1. Find and read an article or letter about a person or a group that has done something helpful for another person, a group, or the general public.

2. Describe *what* they did and explain *why* you think they did it. Would you, could you have done what they did?

   What

   Why

3. Find an example in today's paper of someone or some group that needs help. *What* is their need? *Who* should respond?

Bonus!

How might a newspaper help
- the poor?
- the lonely?
- the ill?

Ever tried to snuggle up to a newspaper?

Copyright © 1984 by Dale Seymour Publications

Newsschool
LEARNING FROM LIFE

DESIRE & DETERMINATION

1. While reading today's sports stories, look for examples of athletes who have done unusual things to prepare themselves for competition.

2. List the name, the event, and the training preparation. Include the amount of time and the kinds of sacrifices individuals make to be winners.

Name	Event	Training & Effort

Bonus!

Which would you guess is the real secret to any success?
- a specific goal
- self-discipline

Do you have to fall asleep before you can dream?

Newsschool
LEARNING FROM LIFE

GOOD SPORTS

1. Select a major story in today's sports section and underline statements inside quotation marks. Read carefully to make sure you know who is making each statement.

2. Place a red check mark beside the statements made by the winning side and a blue check mark beside the statements made by the losing side.

3. Copy the parts of the winners' statements that indicate good sportsmanship. Are there other ways that the winners show that they are "good sports"?

4. Copy the parts of the losers' statements that indicate good sportsmanship. How else did the losers appear to be "good sports"? What would *you* have said or done?

Bonus!

If you were a coach, what advice would you usually give a loser?

Next time...

Copyright © 1984 by Dale Seymour Publications

Newsschool
LEARNING FROM LIFE

SUCCESS

1. Find an article in today's paper about a person who succeeded in getting something he/she wanted.

   Miss America from small town

2. Name the person and the achievement.
   Name any other people involved in the success and explain their involvement.

3. What would you say was the *one* most important key in this person's success? Explain briefly.

4. What do you want most to accomplish this year? How can you use that same key for your own success story?

Bonus! Unscramble this word and discover another key to success: S E D E R I

You gotta have heart.

86 Copyright © 1984 by Dale Seymour Publications

Newsschool
LEARNING FROM LIFE

WHAT FAMILIES ARE FOR

1. Find and cut out an article in today's paper that involves a family: parents, children, relatives.

2. List the family members, and tell how and why each member is involved or affected by the events described in the story.

3. Who would you say is the *most important* family member in this story? Why?

4. Does this story make you appreciate something about your own home and family? Explain.

Bonus!

What does family mean to you? Think of a word or phrase for each letter:

F A M I L Y

Father and Mother I Love You!

Copyright © 1984 by Dale Seymour Publications

Newsschool
LEARNING FROM LIFE

PERSONAL PROFILES

1. Find and cut out the picture and story of a person featured in today's paper.

2. Circle the words in the story that *describe* the person.

3. Underline statements *by* the person or *about* the person that reveal his/her attitudes, values, and personality.

4. Write a paragraph telling why you *would* or *would not* like to be this person's good friend.

Bonus!

Are *character* qualities and *personality* the same or different? Explain.

It's what's inside that counts...

Newsschool
LEARNING FROM LIFE

VIRTUES OF A VALENTINE

1. Find in today's paper an example of these qualities:

   a. Who in today's paper has great *courage*?

   b. Who in today's paper best demonstrates your idea of true *love*?

   c. Who in today's paper seems to have great *wisdom*?

   d. Who in today's paper has the best *sense of humor*?

2. Explain why you feel the persons you chose qualify for the virtue they represent.

Bonus!

What are the *four cardinal virtues* and what do they mean?

"Must be the opposite of the cardinal sins!"

Copyright © 1984 by Dale Seymour Publications

Newsschool
LEARNING FROM LIFE

MOTHER'S DAY

1. Find and cut out of today's paper words and pictures that remind you of your mother when she is at her very best.

2. Fold a large piece of construction paper like a greeting card. Try out a variety of arrangements with your words and pictures until the best ones fit into an organization you really like. Glue the words and pictures in place.

3. Of all the items you found, highlight in some way the three or four that you like the *most* in your mother, then give her the card.

Bonus!

Find Mother Goose in an encyclopedia. Who was she and where did she come from?

Web-footed Bertha??!

Newsschool
LEARNING FROM LIFE

FATHER'S DAY

1. Find and cut out of today's paper words and pictures that make you think of "father." Arrange the words and pictures attractively on one side of a large sheet of construction paper.

optimist   **SPORT**   **best**

2. Circle the four words or pictures that *best symbolize* your feelings about "father." List the four items on the back and explain why you chose each one

3. Draw a box around the word on the front that is *most important* for a father. On the back explain why that word is most important.

Bonus!

What are "paternal grandparents"?

Good patterns...?

Copyright © 1984 by Dale Seymour Publications

Newsschool
LEARNING FROM LIFE

THE WAY I SEE ME...

Oboy.. Aghh! Hmm.. OK!

Make a collection of words and pictures in today's paper that describe the way you see yourself *now* and five years in the *future*. Write a paragraph about how you are using the present to make your future come true.

PRESENT	FUTURE

Bonus!

"You are becoming whatever you will be."
Agree/Disagree
Why?

I am what I've been??!

YESTERDAY — TODAY — TOMORROW

Newsschool
LEARNING FROM LIFE

FREE ADVICE

1. Find in today's paper letters people have written asking for advice or help with health, family, or social problems.

2. Select one letter and underline the words that best state the problem.

3. Circle the words that reveal how the person *feels* about the problem.

4. What would you have said to answer the letter? Do you agree or disagree with the advice given?

Bonus!

Why does the President need a whole staff of advisors?

Because he needs all the advice he can get!

Newsschool
LEARNING FROM LIFE

CANDID COMICS

1. Find a comic strip in today's paper that shows someone doing or saying something that in *real life* would be considered "unusual behavior."

2. If *you* were to do the same thing in real life, how do you think people would react?

3. Find a news article that describes *unusual behavior*. Is there humor in the real life situation? Give reasons for your answer.

Bonus!

When did Dagwood and Blondie get married in Chic Young's comic?

Well... they don't really act like newlyweds...

Newsschool
LEARNING FROM LIFE

LAUGHING MATTER

1. Cut out of today's paper any two comic strips or cartoons that make you laugh. Study the types of humor listed in this activity to see what produces humor in the cartoons you selected.

2. For each cartoon explain what creates the humor. Change a word or an action to show where humor actually occurs in the cartoon.

TYPES OF HUMOR

___ 1. Unexpected happening (surprise)
___ 2. Unlikely happening (incongruity)
___ 3. Words with double meaning (puns)
___ 4. Twisting, exaggeration, or distortion of truth
___ 5. Interrupted repetition
___ 6. Faulty comparison or contrast
___ 7. Oversimplification or overstatement

Bonus!

Which form of humor is most unkind?
- wit
- satire
- sarcasm

And it's the easiest to produce...

Copyright © 1984 by Dale Seymour Publications

Newsschool
LEARNING FROM LIFE

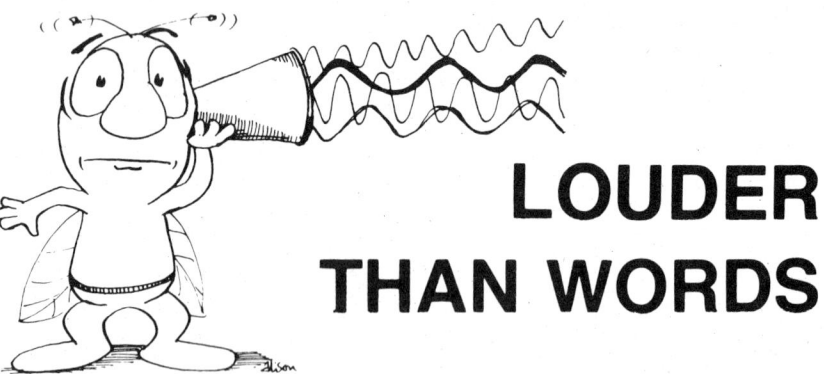

LOUDER THAN WORDS

1. Find an ad in today's paper that appears to be "shouting" at you. What did the ad designer do to make the ad "loud"?

2. Find a cartoon character in today's paper whose *face* and *body* convey anger or fear. How did the cartoonist create that effect?

3. Find an ad in today's paper in which *clothing* helps convey a message of fun, relaxation, leisure, and play.

4. Find an ad that makes you *feel* excited, angry, elegant, or serious. Analyze the ad to see what was all working together to create that feeling in you.

Bonus!

Which of these is most important to advertisers?
(1) Get the reader to act.
(2) Hold the reader's interest.
(3) Get the reader's attention.

Consumer beware...!

EAT AT JOE'S

Newsschool
LEARNING FROM LIFE

LETTERING

1. Find and cut out of today's ads 15 words, each lettered in a different style.

2. Choose three different lettering styles and explain how the lettering style helps convey a message in the ad.

3. Select any one of the 15 styles and use the same style of lettering to write your name below.

Bonus!

Calligraphy is:
a. the art of dancing.
b. the art of handwriting.
c. the art of painting.

The art of spelling?

Newsschool
LEARNING FROM LIFE

LINE DRAWINGS

1. Create a straight-line design by coloring any of the lines on a classified ad page.

2. Find an attractive ad in today's paper that fits each description:
   a. Mostly straight lines.
   b. Mostly curved lines.
   c. Both straight and curved lines.

3. Find an ad that suggests *boldness* and *strength* with heavy lines.
   Find an ad that suggests *daintiness* or *elegance* with fine lines.

Bonus!

*What does a broken line around an ad usually mean?

Some graphic artist had the jitters!

98 Copyright © 1984 by Dale Seymour Publications

Newsschool
LEARNING FROM LIFE

CREATIVE CREATIONS

1. Find and cut out of today's paper four unusual (or interesting) arrangements of words, color, lines, symbols, shapes, or objects.

2. Explain what the artist has done to create an interesting and/or unusual effect.

3. Create an artistic arrangement of your own with words, lines, symbols, pictures, or shapes cut from any place in today's paper. What is the theme or message of your creation?

Bonus!

What are graffiti?
a. the bits of paper you throw at parades
b. writings on a wall
c. pasta in an Italian casserole

If I have to eat any words, I'd prefer them in a casserole...

Copyright © 1984 by Dale Seymour Publications

Newsschool
LEARNING FROM LIFE

COLOR ADDED

1. Find two large advertisements in today's paper that use no color.

2. Draw a line from top to bottom to divide each ad in half. Color half of each ad with color crayons.

3. Find one ad in today's paper that uses color. Reproduce half of the ad in black and white.

4. Suggest 3 reasons why color is often used to attract readers and buyers.

Bonus!

Circle the 3 basic colors:
- red
- blue
- green
- orange
- brown
- yellow

Black, white, and grey.

100 Copyright © 1984 by Dale Seymour Publications

Newsschool
LEARNING FROM LIFE

WARM & COOL COLORS

1. Cut out several color ads in today's paper. Sort the ads by those that use reds and yellows (warm colors) and those that use blues and greens (cool colors).

2. Is there any relationship between the colors used and the items advertised? Why did the advertiser choose warm or cool colors to advertise the items to be sold?

3. Select two large black and white ads from today's paper. Color one with warm colors and the other with cool colors.

4. Which ads get your attention faster?
   ☐ warm colored ads
   ☐ cool colored ads

Bonus!

Which is a warm feeling and which is a cool feeling?

"He saw red!"
"He was green with envy."

The trembling and cold chills should be a clue...

ENVY

Copyright © 1984 by Dale Seymour Publications

Newsschool
LEARNING FROM LIFE

SIGN LANGUAGE

1. Find and cut out of today's paper at least five pictures or drawings (not words) that represent a specific business, idea, or product.

2. Label each symbol and tell what it communicates.

3. Study the history and development of *trademarks*. Write a brief report on trademarks as an art form, as an element of culture, and as an efficient form of communication.

Bonus!

What nationwide trademark is represented by two overlapping circles of red and gold?

In fact, it's used far too often...

Newsschool
LEARNING FROM LIFE

TRADEMARKS

1. Cut out 10 trademarks in today's paper.
   A "trademark" is the artistic combination of pictures, words, letters, symbols, and style that represent a particular business or product.

2. Which two of the 10 trademarks you chose have the most impressive combination of words, symbols, and styles? Explain the *reasons* for your two choices.

3. Design a trademark for yourself that symbolizes what you feel is unique about you.

Bonus!

What does this symbol mean in an ad?

VISA

It's easy to fall in debt...

Copyright © 1984 by Dale Seymour Publications

103

Newsschool
LEARNING FROM LIFE

THE ART OF PERSUADING

1. Find and read newspaper stories about problems, crimes, and accidents.

   As you read, *imagine a new product or service* that could be advertised and sold to solve the problem, stop the crime, or prevent the accident.

   Name the product or service.

2. Draw and/or describe the product or service you would sell. What would it be like? How would it work? Who would buy it? How much would it cost?

3. Design an ad that will convince people that they need and want what you have to sell.

Bonus!

Who invented the first bicycle?
A Frenchman?
A German?
An Englishman?
An American?

Psst! It was called a célérifère!

104 Copyright © 1984 by Dale Seymour Publications

Newsschool
LEARNING FROM LIFE

LOOKS ON FACES

1. Cut out 20 faces in today's paper and group them into categories by how the faces seem to feel:
   - happy
   - sad
   - bored
   - worried
   - amused
   - angry

2. Which category has the most faces in it? Is it true that *most* people feel that feeling most often? Explain your answer.

3. Find an article that interests you and draw four faces for emotions expressed in the article. Tell who the face is and the situation creating the feeling.

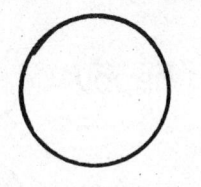

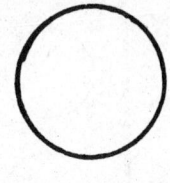

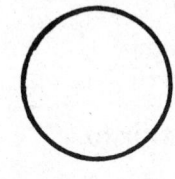

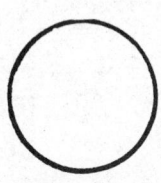

   Person _____ _____ _____ _____
   Situation _____ _____ _____ _____

Bonus!

When your "feelings get hurt," which emotion is most common?
a. anger
b. sadness
c. embarrassment

d. All of the above...

Copyright © 1984 by Dale Seymour Publications

105

Newsschool
LEARNING FROM LIFE

MASKS

1. Find two faces in today's paper that look happy. What parts of the face reveal the happiness?
   ___ mouth
   ___ nose
   ___ eyes

2. Find two sad faces in today's paper. Which parts of the face are most expressive?
   ___ mouth
   ___ nose
   ___ eyes

3. Find a cartoon character to match these expressions.
   ___ anger
   ___ surprise
   ___ fear
   ___ uncertainty

4. Using these circles, draw masks to match these feelings.
   ◯ happy
   ◯ sad
   ◯ mad
   ◯ surprised

Bonus!

Describe the kind of person you expect to find behind this mask:

Boo!

106 Copyright © 1984 by Dale Seymour Publications

Newsschool
LEARNING FROM LIFE

COSTUMES

1. Find and cut out a head-to-toe picture or illustration of a man, woman, a teenager, and a child from today's paper.

2. How old would you guess each person is? What kinds of activities would each person do?

3. What is each person wearing that is characteristic of his/her age and activities?

4. Find 2 other "costumes" in today's paper. What does each "costume" tell you about the one who would wear it?

Bonus!

What is the difference between "costumes" and "uniforms"?

Costumes are scratchier...

Copyright © 1984 by Dale Seymour Publications

107

Newsschool
LEARNING FROM LIFE

CHARACTERS

1. Find a drawing of a character in today's paper that represents a certain person, a particular job, or a specific type of activity.

2. Explain what the artist did to the picture to make it easy for you to recognize the person, the job, or the activity.

3. Find a definition of the word "stereotype." Find a stereotyped version of a "woman" and a "man" in today's paper.

4. What similarities of women in general and men in general is the artist exaggerating in each example? What differences is the artist ignoring in each of your examples?

Bonus!

What are the 'masks' and 'costumes' for these characters?
- housewife
- teenager
- businessman

The universal symbol of servitude...

Newsschool
LEARNING FROM LIFE

LIVELY BODIES

1. Find and cut out 5 pictures or illustrations in today's paper of people doing various kinds of activities.

2. Draw a stick figure over each pictured person. Notice how a stick figure can easily change from one position to another.

3. Choose a comic strip character to draw. Begin with a stick figure to get the right position. Then add width and weight to fill out the body.

4. Can you draw Bug by using this method?

   (Bug is the guy pictured below. He's also juggling in the picture above.)

Bonus!

Fill in the blanks with vowels to make another title for this activity.

_ N _ M _ T _ D
_ N _ T _ M _ _ S

Psst... Both words start with the first vowel!

Copyright © 1984 by Dale Seymour Publications

Newsschool
LEARNING FROM LIFE

TRICKS & TECHNIQUES

1. Select and cut out two of your favorite humorous comic strips from today's paper.

2. Study the expressions on each face. What did the cartoonist do to show the _feelings_ of the characters?

3. Study the bodies of the characters. What did the cartoonist do with heads, arms, legs, and feet to tell the reader something?

4. How has the cartoonist created humor? What makes the strip funny? Is the humor in the words, the art, or both?

Bonus!

What do these two pairs of eyes say?

A   B

Let's hear it for a nose.

110 Copyright © 1984 by Dale Seymour Publications

Newsschool
LEARNING FROM LIFE

KINDS OF CARTOONS

1. Find one example of each of these four kinds of cartoons in today's newspaper.
   a. Editorial cartoon—a cartoon about a political, social, or economic situation.
   b. Comic strip—a series of cartoon panels that tell a story.
   c. Gag cartoon—the single cartoon with a one-line statement.
   d. Illustrative cartoons—cartoons used with a story or advertising to attract and interest readers.

2. Why is each cartoon more effective than a photograph taken to show the same idea would be?

3. Why is each cartoon more effective than a story or essay about the same idea would be?

Bonus!

Which of these famous cartoonists is best known for his editorial cartoons?
- Charles Shultz
- Bill Mauldin
- Hank Ketcham

How about the editorial comic strip?

Copyright © 1984 by Dale Seymour Publications

Newsschool
LEARNING FROM LIFE

DETAILS, DETAILS

1. Find a comic strip in today's paper that repeats the same figures or backgrounds through several frames.

2. Look closely. Are the figures and background drawn the same for each frame or are there subtle differences in details: wider lines, narrower stripes, something missing, something added?

3. Design 3 questions about the strip's details and see if another person is as aware of details as you are.

Bonus! Find the artist's initials in the cartoon at the *top* of this activity.

"I've got her underfoot..."

112 Copyright © 1984 by Dale Seymour Publications

Newsschool
LEARNING FROM LIFE

SLIGHT (?!) EXAGGERATIONS!

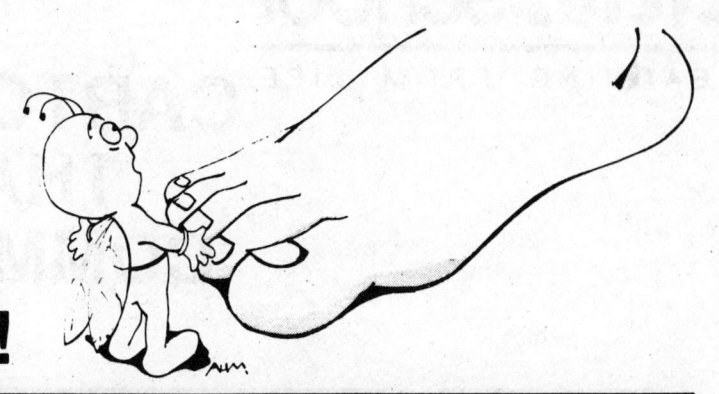

1. Find and cut out the editorial cartoons in today's paper.

   Who are the *people* represented in each cartoon?

2. What are the *symbols* in each cartoon and what do they represent?

3. Look for *exaggeration* in each cartoon. What is much larger, or smaller, or in any other way a distortion of reality?

4. What is the message the cartoonist wants to say through the characters, the symbols, and the exaggeration?

Bonus!

What is the difference between a caricature and a portrait?

A bit of truth...

Copyright © 1984 by Dale Seymour Publications

Newsschool
LEARNING FROM LIFE

CARTOONS THAT COMMENT

1. Find and cut out one of the editorial cartoons from today's editorial page.

2. Who are the *people* represented in the cartoon?

   What are the *symbols* and what do they represent?

3. List two *facts* illustrated in the cartoon.

   List two *opinions* illustrated in the cartoon.

4. State in one well-developed sentence the main idea that the artist wants to convey through the cartoon.

Bonus!

What is Thomas Nast famous for?

"For starting a fad..."

Newsschool
LEARNING FROM LIFE

CARTOON COMPARISONS

1. Find and cut out two editorial cartoons from today's editorial pages. What is the topic of each cartoon?

2. For each cartoon explain the likenesses the artist is suggesting between the real situation and the cartoon situation.

	TOPIC	REAL LIFE SITUATION
Cartoon #1		
Cartoon #2		

Bonus!

An ANALOGY points out:
    a. the differences.
    b. the similarities.
    c. the unusual.

It usually points out how little I know!

Copyright © 1984 by Dale Seymour Publications

Newsschool
LEARNING FROM LIFE

OPINIONATED PICTURES

1. Find a news article in today's paper on a topic about which you have strong feelings and opinions.

2. For that topic identify all of the following:

   a. **Main characters**

   _____
   _____

   b. **Symbols**

   _____
   _____

   c. **Activities**

   _____
   _____

3. Draw an editorial cartoon showing how you think the characters, symbols, and activities are related.

Bonus!

Which appeared first, the editorial cartoon or the comic strip?

The characters!

Newsschool
LEARNING FROM LIFE

FOTO FACTS

1. Cut out of today's paper 3 large news photos. For each photo, list *facts* shown in the picture.

2. Can you *prove* the facts you have listed? Are you assuming certain things to be true or are you absolutely positive? Explain.

3. Select one of the pictures and list some ideas and feelings you get from it about the relationships, attitudes, and backgrounds of the people involved.

Bonus!

Which is more likely to be true to life: a posed photo or a candid photo?

Ever tried to be candid while posing??

Copyright © 1984 by Dale Seymour Publications

Newsschool
LEARNING FROM LIFE

JUST PICTURE THAT!

1. Cut out a story in today's paper that includes a picture. List some things you *know* just by looking at the picture.

   I know:

2. Read the story and add to your list new things you learned that the picture did not tell.

   Now I know:

Bonus!

Name two *disadvantages* of TV news. Name two *advantages*.

"It interrupts my fun, for one thing!"